# THINKING ABOUT EDUCATION SERIES
### FIFTH EDITION
**Jonas F. Soltis,** *Editor*

The revised and expanded Fifth Edition of this series builds on the strengths of the previous editions. Written in a clear and concise style, these books speak directly to preservice and in-service teachers. Each offers useful interpretive categories and thought-provoking insights into daily practice in schools. Numerous case studies provide a needed bridge between theory and practice. Basic philosophical perspectives on teaching, learning, curriculum, ethics, and the relation of school to society are made readily accessible to the reader.

### PERSPECTIVES ON LEARNING
D. C. Phillips and Jonas F. Soltis

### THE ETHICS OF TEACHING
Kenneth A. Strike and Jonas F. Soltis

### CURRICULUM AND AIMS
Decker F. Walker and Jonas F. Soltis

### SCHOOL AND SOCIETY
Walter Feinberg and Jonas F. Soltis

### APPROACHES TO TEACHING
Gary D Fenstermacher and Jonas F. Soltis

THINKING ABOUT EDUCATION SERIES

5TH EDITION

# THE ETHICS OF TEACHING

KENNETH A. STRIKE

JONAS F. SOLTIS

Teachers College
Columbia University
New York and London

Published by Teachers College Press, 1234 Amsterdam Avenue, New York, NY 10027

Copyright © 2009 by Teachers College, Columbia University

*Library of Congress Cataloging-in-Publication Data*

Strike, Kenneth A.
 The ethics of teaching / Kenneth A. Strike, Jonas F. Soltis. — 5th ed.
     p. cm. — (Thinking about education series)
 Includes bibliographical references and index.
 ISBN 978-0-8077-4981-4 (pbk. : alk. paper)
 1. College teachers—Professional ethics—United States. I. Soltis, Jonas F.
II. Title.
 LB1779.S73 2009
 378.1'25—dc22                                                    2009000215

ISBN 978-0-8077-4981-4  (paper)

Printed on acid-free paper

Manufactured in the United States of America

16   15   14   13   12   11   10   09        8   7   6   5   4   3   2   1

# Contents

132412

# Acknowledgments

We would like to thank The Hasting Center Institute of Society, Ethics, and the Life Sciences for bringing us together and starting us thinking about the ethics of teaching at a conference entitled "Professional Ethics in Schools of Education" held in October 1981. We must also thank the many students who attended our classes and helped us to develop and test our approach and materials in Education 472 (Cornell) and TF4680 (Teachers College, Columbia). Some students were kind enough to let us use cases they had constructed: Randy Berger, Tim Counihan, Ann Marie Kelley, Meg Lavigne, Karley Meltzer, Barbara Reynolds, Scott Smith, and Steve Tobolsky. We also had the benefit of seeing some of the cases developed in the Ohio State project on Moral Negotiation. For that we thank Bernard Rosen, Gerald Reagan, and Jo Ann Freiberg. Very special thanks go to Andrew Alexander, Paul Green, and Tim Counihan, who served as research assistants doing everything including finding sources, copy editing, and offering suggestions. Tim Counihan, who was with the project from start to finish, also ably assisted in ethics courses at Teachers College and skillfully developed and edited cases, some of which appear in this text. Jo Ellen Thomas and Berni Oltz prepared the manuscript, asked some very good questions, and made useful suggestions. Many people read and commented on the manuscript. Among them were Barry Bull, Scott Bilow, Martha Cummings, James Galt, Emil Haller, John Decker, Charles Love, Naomi Mascarenhas, Margaret McCasland, Karley Meltzer, David Monk, George Posner, Vern Rockcastle, Merrill Stevenson, Abebetch Tadesse, Craig Thurtell, and Michael Weinstock.

We also would like to thank Tom Rotell, former Director of Teachers College Press, and Carole Saltz, the current Director, who supported and encouraged the development of this series, Thinking About Education, as well as Sarah Biondello, former Executive Acquisitions Editor, who encouraged the second edition and involved Teachers College Press in additional books on ethics and education. Finally, we thank Susan Liddicoat and Peter Sieger of Teachers College Press for the overseeing and caretaking of all the subsequent editions of the series.

# Code of Ethics of the Education Profession

## Adopted by the 1975 NEA Representative Assembly

### PREAMBLE

The educator, believing in the worth and dignity of each human being, recognizes the supreme importance of the pursuit of truth, devotion to excellence, and the nurture of democratic principles. Essential to these goals is the protection of freedom to learn and to teach and the guarantee of equal educational opportunity for all. The educator accepts the responsibility to adhere to the highest ethical standards.

The educator recognizes the magnitude of the responsibility inherent in the teaching process. The desire for the respect and confidence of one's colleagues, of students, of parents, and of the members of the community provides the incentive to attain and maintain the highest possible degree of ethical conduct. The Code of Ethics of the Education Profession indicates the aspiration of all educators and provides standards by which to judge conduct.

The remedies specified by the NEA and/or its affiliates for the violation of any provision of this Code shall be exclusive and no such provision shall be enforceable in any form other than one specifically designated by the NEA or its affiliates.

---

Reprinted from *NEA Handbook, 1977-78*, Washington, DC: National Education Association. Used by permission.

## PRINCIPLE 1

### Commitment to the Student

The educator strives to help each student realize his or her potential as a worthy and effective member of society. The educator therefore works to stimulate the spirit of inquiry, the acquisition of knowledge and understanding, and the thoughtful formulation of worthy goals.

In fulfillment of the obligation to the student, the educator—

1   Shall not unreasonably restrain the student from independent action in the pursuit of learning.
2   Shall not unreasonably deny the student access to varying points of view.
3.  Shall not deliberately suppress or distort subject matter relevant to the student's progress.
4.  Shall make reasonable effort to protect the student from conditions harmful to learning or to health and safety.
5.  Shall not intentionally expose the student to embarrassment or disparagement.
6.  Shall not on the basis of race, color, creed, sex, national origin, marital status, political or religious beliefs, family, social or cultural background, or sexual orientation, unfairly:
    a.  Exclude any student from participation in any program;
    b.  Deny benefits to any student;
    c.  Grant any advantage to any student.
7.  Shall not use professional relationships with students for private advantage.
8.  Shall not disclose information about students obtained in the course of professional service, unless disclosure serves a compelling professional purpose or is required by law.

## PRINCIPLE II

### Commitment to the Profession

The education profession is vested by the public with a trust and responsibility requiring the highest ideals of professional service.

In the belief that the quality of the services of the education profession directly influences the nation and its citizens, the educator shall exert every effort to raise professional standards, to promote a climate that encourages the exercise of professional judgment, to achieve conditions which attract persons worthy of the trust to careers in education, and to assist in preventing the practice of the profession by unqualified persons.

In fulfillment of the obligations to the profession, the educator—

1. Shall not in an application for a professional position deliberately make a false statement or fail to disclose a material fact related to competency and qualifications.
2. Shall not misrepresent his/her professional qualifications.
3. Shall not assist entry into the profession of a person known to be unqualified in respect to character, education, or other relevant attribute.
4. Shall not knowingly make a false statement concerning the qualifications of a candidate for a professional position.
5. Shall not assist a noneducator in the unauthorized practice of teaching.
6. Shall not disclose information about colleagues obtained in the course of professional service unless disclosure serves a compelling professional purpose or is required by law.
7. Shall not knowingly make false or malicious statements about a colleague.
8. Shall not accept any activity, gift, or favor that might impair or appear to influence professional decisions or actions.

*Chapter 1*

---

# What This Book Is About

This is a book about the ethics of teaching. You already may know that there is a code of ethics for educators. In fact, the National Education Association Code appears at the beginning of this book. But we are less concerned with your learning the code than in getting you to think about ethics and educating on your own. Ethical thinking and decision making are not just following the rules.

To get you in the right frame of mind and to see what this book is about, let us start with an imaginary situation that could have occurred just as easily on your campus as in our imaginations. As you read it, try to put yourself in the place of the young beginning instructor and ask yourself what would you have done if you were she.

Cynthia Allen was a new instructor in the English department and not much older than her students. She took on the task of teaching the required introductory literature and composition courses with zest and with hours and hours of careful class preparation. However, like many beginning teachers, she soon learned that enthusiasm, hard work, and planning are not always guarantees of success. Some students were bright and performed very well in class. She thought they probably would do just as well no matter who taught the course. Other students, however, did not seem to learn what she tried so hard to teach them. Their work was average or below average, and they sat in the classroom with little to say. She did not know if these students were lost or bored or did not understand her, but she knew that any improvement in this group would please her very much and mark her success as a beginning instructor—if she could only reach them.

The course requirements were four short essays and a final term paper. Cynthia thought this would be a fair evaluation system because it allowed for improvement if a student had not done well at first. The final papers were due on the last day of class, and all the students dutifully handed them in. Having said good-bye to her home-for-the-holidays-bound students, Cynthia turned to the task of reading the final papers and calculating course grades, which were due in the registrar's office within 48 hours.

Reading the first paper, she received a great surprise: Henry, an important new member of the college basketball team, had shown remarkable improvement in his work. Cynthia had found him to be an earnest student during the term, but his schedule of practice and travel made it difficult for him to keep up with classwork. His earlier grades had been D, D+, C–, and C. She knew it was necessary for Henry to maintain a C average in order to remain eligible for intercollegiate sports and to retain his scholarship. She read his final paper with great concern and hope that soon turned to joy and surprise. It clearly was an A paper!

In fact, it was so good that in order to comment on it intelligently, Cynthia had to consult a standard reference book on the topic. There, again to her surprise, she discovered Henry had copied much of his paper directly from the text. It was a clear case of plagiarism.

In addition to a sense of hurt, anger, and failure, Cynthia realized she now had an obligation to the institution. The policy on academic dishonesty was clear:

> The penalty for a proven case of academic dishonesty is an F in the course. No provision can be made for a student's withdrawal. The faculty member alleging dishonesty will notify, in writing, the student, the dean of students, and the faculty member's department chairperson. Such notification will become part of the dean's official file on the student but will not be transmitted outside the university.

The policy on cheating was clear, but Cynthia had some doubts. She was not sure such harsh measures were appropriate in this case or would accomplish desirable educational goals. Following normal procedures would seem to result in a very drastic penalty. If reported and proven to be cheating, Henry would lose his scholarship and probably have to leave school; and the basketball team would lose a valuable player just at tournament time. For other students, one F might not be such a burden. For Henry it would be a disaster. What would you do if you were Cynthia?

Stop for a moment and think about this predicament. If you can, discuss it with your roommate or a classmate. If you could take some time to think and talk about it, it would soon become dear that a number of ethical principles and values are at issue here: honesty and dishonesty on the part of both the student and the instructor; obligations to an institution whose rules one presumably agrees to follow by becoming a member, either as a student or as a faculty member; concern for a student's well-being and the recognition of students as persons with lives outside the classroom and with futures that teachers can influence beyond measure.

There are a number of issues and options to unravel. The NEA code does not seem to be of much help, lacking an explicit rule to cover this situation. Implicitly it seems to take the position that teachers should act toward students with the welfare of the student as their primary concern. It also generally requires that teachers act honestly and with integrity in professional matters. Ordinarily we would all agree that honesty and the student's welfare are important values. But when they CLash, as they do in this case, then consulting a code or agreeing on values will not help in deciding what to do as much as will some hard ethical thinking—and that is what this book will help you understand how to do.

If Cynthia does not fail Henry and report him because she feels the punishment is too great in this case, she would be paying more attention in her thinking to the harmful consequences of her actions than to the obligation she has to obey the rules. In this book we will call such ethical thinking consequentialist. If, however, she takes seriously her personal sense of honesty and her professional obligation to maintain and administer the academic code of her institution fairly to all, she would reach her decision as a nonconsequentialist, one for whom duty, obligation, and principle are more important considerations than consequences.

By using case studies like this one, we will explore ethical problems in teaching that center around the ideas of punishment, intellectual freedom, and equality in the treatment of students. When reading them, you will have to use your imagination and project yourself into the role of the teacher. Then you will have to do some hard ethical thinking yourself. You should also try imagining that you are the student in these cases. Sometimes ethical considerations look different from the perspective of a different person in the situation. In the above case, try imagining you are Henry, a talented minority student with a sick mother who sees his only chance to make something of his life in becoming a professional basketball player. For Henry, it is a case of staying in school with a shot at the pros or going back to the ghetto and a life of menial labor or chronic unemployment. How would you support your diabetic widowed mother? You have a D+/C– average going into the final paper. You have to pull a high grade to get your average up to stay in school and play bail. You know that treating a source as if it were your own work is wrong, but you have been improving and honestly passing the course so far. What would you do?

Using case studies will help put you in a thinking mood. In this book we will use them extensively to display ethical theories and ways of ethical thinking and to present cases for you and your classmates to grapple with on your own. The case studies in Chapters 2–4 will supply a context for understanding some major ways ethical theorists have thought about the issues of punishment, freedom, and equality. We will also treat ethical issues related to democracy and cultural diversity in Chapters 5 and 6.

These chapters will follow a simple pattern designed to inform and challenge your thinking. First, there will be a "Case" that, like the case of Cynthia Allen in this chapter, sets up the ethical dilemma. Next, there will be an imaginary "Dispute" that lays out some of the ethical issues of the case in an intuitive way. Disputes will be similar to the kinds of discussions that occur in a dorm room or in a teachers' lounge when people sense something is morally amiss and argue over what is ethically problematic. This will give you a feeling for what is at issue. Then a discussion of ethical "Concepts" relevant to the dilemma will provide an opportunity for you to see how major ethical theories throw some light on the issues. These theories will deal not only with what is to be considered right or wrong, but also with how we can decide what is right or wrong. Understanding the thinking of major ethical theorists will help you see some options open to you as an ethical thinker. In the next section, called "Analysis," we will show you what it would be like to think about and reach a decision using the consequentialist and the nonconsequentialist perspectives, as well as the principles of respect for persons and benefit maximization. We will also reflect on the nature of ethical thinking itself. Finally, at the end of each chapter and in the last part of the book we will provide additional case studies for class discussions.

But before we begin our treatment of cases, it is important to make you aware that this book also treats another theme that is very crucial to contemporary thinking about professional ethics and ethics in general. Most people probably would agree that teachers should behave in an ethical manner. Many people also might have serious doubts that questions about ethical behavior can be settled objectively. Perhaps you are one of those people. "After all," you might say, "aren't questions of ethics really questions of personal values or the values of the group to which one belongs?" "Is there really an objective right or wrong in human affairs?" "Doesn't it really just come down to what one believes is right or wrong?" "Isn't it wrong for one person to try to impose his or her values on someone else?"

We are aware that subjectivism and relativism are serious contemporary concerns. To the modern ear, the claim that one should do such and such because it is the right thing to do sounds intolerant and dogmatic. Why should someone else's opinion be better than yours? Can we be tolerant without being relativistic? Can we be objective without being certain? These are disturbing, but important, considerations that no serious discussion of ethics today can avoid.

Therefore, we believe that if we are to be successful in getting you to think effectively about professional ethics, we will have to persuade you that questions of ethics can be objectively discussed and morally justified courses of action undertaken. In what follows, we shall try to do just that, but ultimately you must be the judge. We believe that a kind of rational ethical thinking that goes beyond personal beliefs and values is essential both to professional ethics and to the moral education of all members of society. Ethics is a public as well as a personal matter. If we are correct, then it would seem to follow that teachers have a special obligation to help their students see and share the potential objectivity and rationality of ethical thinking so that we can all lead morally responsible lives together. That is also what this book is about.

## THE NATURE OF ETHICAL INQUIRY

The Code of Ethics of the National Education Association contains the following statement: "The educator ... shall not deliberately suppress or distort subject matter relevant to the student's progress." All of us probably believe this. It certainly seems wrong to lie to or deceive students. One might quibble, of course. Is it always wrong? How are we to decide when deliberate distortion has occurred? We suspect, however, that there will be few who will wish to defend the general merits of deceiving students, no matter what their quibbles may be.

We also suspect that agreement can be reached on another claim about this statement. It is an ethical statement. It is not a description of what the world is like. Instead, it tells us what we ought to do.

These observations about this statement from the NEA Code raise two questions. First, what makes this claim an ethical one, and, second, how do we know that it is true? Let us start with the first question.

What makes a claim an ethical claim? To answer that, we need to know what ethics is about. Some obvious things come to mind. Ethics concerns what kinds of actions are right or wrong, what kind of life is a good life, or what kind of person is a good person. All of these things seem clear enough. Our thinking will be advanced, however, if we can distinguish ethical claims from two other sorts of claims.

Ethical claims need first to be distinguished from factual ones. Facts tell us something about the world. They describe. They are true when the world is the way they say it is. Otherwise they are false. The claim "the world is round" is true because the world is round, and the claim "the world is flat" is false because the world is round. Claims about what is right and wrong seem not to describe in this way. They are not true because they correctly describe some part of the world. They do not tell us how the world is, but how it ought to be. Thus they prescribe, not describe. When someone behaves in a way that is different from how people ought to behave, an ethical standard is violated, but that standard does not become false because the world turns out to be different from that which is prescribed. That people sometimes lie or steal does not falsify the duty to be honest.

Because moral claims are not facts does not mean that they cannot be true or false, however. It only means that they cannot be true or false in the same way that facts are. We do not decide if ethical claims are true or false by seeing if they correspond to the world. How we do decide if they are true or false is a story for later.

It is also important to distinguish ethical claims from appraisals or preferences. Perhaps the need to do this is not obvious. Most of us are used to thinking of ethical judgments, appraisals, and preferences as "values." Nevertheless, an example may suggest why it is useful to distinguish ethical claims from these other kinds of "values." Suppose I have a friend who is an excellent skier. One day as I see him flying down the slope, I remark, "My, he's a good skier." Now think how odd it would be to treat this remark as a comment about his character, as though I had said, "My, he's a good person." The word good is a general word of appraisal. Sometimes we use it in an ethical way. We do this when we want to approve the rightness of an action or the moral qualities of a person. For example, we are likely to describe individuals who are unusually kind or who devote their lives to helping others as good people. But we can also use good to say that someone excels at something even when we find the activity quite reprehensible on moral grounds. "He's a good burglar" tells us that a person is competent at a form of theft, not that we approve of theft or believe that theft is morally acceptable.

There is one type of value judgment from which it is particularly important to distinguish ethical claims. These are judgments about what we like or want (or what we ought to like or want). These judgments concern preferences. Here, too, a few examples should suggest that judgments about preferences are quite different from ethical judgments. It would be absurd, for example, to treat someone's claim to like ice cream as a claim concerning the morality of ice cream. Conversely, it is quite possible to find doing the right thing distasteful or unpleasant.

We believe that we have a moral obligation to pay our income tax. We nevertheless dislike paying it a great deal. We believe that we have a moral obligation to grade our students fairly, that is, to give them what they deserve. We would prefer to give them all A's. Moral judgments are not, therefore, statements of preference or taste.

What kinds of judgments are they? Fundamentally, they are statements of obligation. Moral judgments tell us what we ought to do and what we ought not to do. They tell us what our duties are. We have insisted that ethical claims are not just statements about what kinds of behavior we like, approve of, or judge to be excellent or competent. We believe that the tendency to lump ethical judgments under the general class of value judgments and then to treat all value judgments alike is the source of much confusion about ethics. People tend to assume that value judgments are subjective matters. Indeed, it is often believed that they are rightfully a matter of free choice on our part. It is then assumed to be wrong to impose our values on others. These ideas are not always true.

Such thoughts about subjectivity and free choice are often true of preferences. Surely, it would be absurd to hold that it is right to like olives and wrong to like pickles. There is no right or wrong about it. Moreover, an olive lover who set out to compel another person to share this taste would surely violate that person's rights. On the other hand, it is equally absurd to think that the question of whether or not one should be honest is like the question of whether or not one should like olives. It makes good sense to tell someone who feels no obligation to be honest that honesty is a duty. Moreover, it is often reasonable to enforce honesty against those who would choose to be dishonest.

All of this is to say we must not be seduced by the label value into thinking that all value judgments are matters of arbitrary choice and that there is no right or wrong about them. That may or may not turn out to be true. We may fail to show that any moral values can be justified. But we should not uncritically assume that they are unjustifiable at the outset because we confuse moral judgments with preferences.

There are other possibly good reasons to be suspicious about the objectivity of ethical judgments. The Scottish philosopher David Hume (1711–1776) provided one powerful argument.[1] It is sometimes called the "is to ought" fallacy. Hume noted that valid arguments have an interesting property. All of the terms that occur in the conclusion of valid arguments are contained in the premises of that argument. We see how this is so in the following standard textbook argument:

> All men are mortal.
> Socrates is a man.
> Therefore, Socrates is mortal.

If the argument were slightly changed, we would see a conclusion that did not follow from the premises in the argument (even though it might be true). Consider:

> All men are mortal.
> Socrates is mortal.
> Therefore, Socrates' dog is mortal.

We cannot reach a valid conclusion about Socrates' dog unless the dog is

---

1. David Hume, *An Inquiry Concerning Human Understanding* (New York: Liberal Arts Press, 1957).

referred to in the premises of the argument. Valid arguments, after all, tell us what follows from our premises; and things only follow if they are there to begin with. Noting this, Hume then pointed out that it is impossible for any argument containing only factual premises to lead validly to a conclusion about what we ought to do. For any such argument has a new idea in the conclusion that was not in the premises—the idea of obligation. "Ought" conclusions, according to Hume, cannot follow from "is" premises.

We need to be clear about what follows from Hume's argument. Hume's argument does not show that ethical knowledge is impossible. What it does show is that ethical knowledge cannot be entirely based on factual knowledge. But what other kind of knowledge is there?

Some philosophers have concluded from this that ethical arguments are possible only if we begin with some initial ethical assumptions. Once we accept some such assumptions, we can use facts to reason to other ethical conclusions. For example, if we begin with the assumption that it is wrong to cause pain, then we can use the factual claim that humiliation causes pain to reason to the conclusion that it is wrong to humiliate people. All ethical arguments, however, begin with an arbitrary and unprovable assumption. If someone, a sadist for example, does not agree with our initial assumption, we have nothing further to say. No argument for the starting point is possible.

This seems very unsatisfactory. Can our ethical conclusions be any better than our premises? Aren't our conclusions just as arbitrary as our initial assumptions? This position seems to lead us to total skepticism. We cannot really know anything in ethics. We can only deliberate with others about what is right and wrong if we already agree with them about our basic assumptions. Perhaps ethical judgments are a matter of personal preference after all.

Before we surrender too quickly to this viewpoint, we should consider what follows from it. Ask yourself if you would be willing to treat some action that you take to be unquestionably evil as a simple difference of taste. We believe that murdering innocent children and putting poison into medicine bottles is wrong. Is that simply an arbitrary assumption on our part, or is it really wrong? Can *we* know it is wrong? Or are we to conclude that the difference between the Hitlers of the world and decent people is merely that they have different preferences?

If the conclusion of skepticism is hard to swallow, perhaps we should try a different approach. Interestingly, even skeptics and ethical relativists, when they are trying to decide what to do rather than being theoretical and philosophical, seem to be willing and able to consider ethical arguments. How do they do this? In our everyday thinking we and they do not simply treat ethical matters as arbitrary. We all devote a good deal of effort to deciding what is right and what ought to be done. Moreover, we often appear to succeed. Are we simply deluded?

We have a proposal to make at this point. Let us defer the question of whether ethics is possible and look at some real ethical disputes. While we are discussing these issues, we can also look aside from time to time to *see how* we are actually proceeding. We can try to describe how we are thinking and what the properties of real ethical arguments are. When we have done this, we can return to the question of whether it is possible to think about ethical issues objectively. It is hot an issue that cannot be settled easily. It will take a lot of thinking and considering. But how we settle it will make an important difference in how we think and act in ethical situations as teachers and as human beings.

## A CASE

Ms. Jones had not met Johnnie's father. She had spoken on the phone to him several times. In fact, she had spoken to him only half an hour ago. She had told him that Johnnie had been in a fight and that she wished to discuss Johnnie's conduct with him.

Johnnie was often in fights. Not that he was a bad kid. He did not pick on other children or deliberately provoke confrontations. He was just a bit excitable. If he ever suspected that he was being laughed at or criticized, he would charge in swinging. He had not damaged anyone yet. In fact, since he was a small child, he was often the loser. Ms. Jones had once asked him to consider the fact that if he attacked less, he would be beaten up less. Johnnie had only given her a wry smile and said, "I'm used to it." As Johnnie's father charged into her office, that "I'm used to it" took on a whole new meaning. Mr. Pugnacious stood in her doorway with his belt in his hand. All 6'5" of him quivered with wrath as he demanded to have his son turned over to him. "I'll teach that little brat to fight in school," he bellowed. "Where is he?"

Ms. Jones quietly responded that she had not called him so that he would beat Johnnie. She merely wanted to discuss his problem. "What's to discuss?" Mr. Pugnacious answered. "This belt will say it all." The odor beginning to fill the room gave reason to suspect that Mr. Pugnacious was not exactly a model of sobriety.

"But Johnnie didn't start it," Ms. Jones blurted out. "He was beaten up by another boy for no reason. I called you to take him home so that the other boy would not get him after school."

This seemed to suggest a new problem to Mr. Pugnacious. Putting on his belt he asked again to see his son. As he and Ms. Jones walked toward

Johnnie's classroom, Mr. Pugnacious began telling Ms. Jones how he planned to teach Johnnie to fight "like a man." Johnnie was to take "no guff off nobody."

Now Ms. Jones began to wonder why she had told Mr. Pugnacious that others had started the fight. She knew that this time the fight had been entirely Johnnie's fault. He had walked into the room obviously upset about something. He had seen several boys in the corner joking. The moment they had broken out laughing, he had charged into the group throwing punches and screaming, "I'll teach you to make fun of me." The boys who were attacked fought back, perhaps too enthusiastically, but they certainly had not started the fight. Ms. Jones found it hard to blame them if they had gotten in a few extra licks.

What really bothered Ms. Jones was that she had lied to Mr. Pugnacious. She considered herself to be an honest person and strongly believed that it was wrong to lie. Indeed, before today, she would very likely have said that lying was always wrong. But she lied to prevent Johnnie from receiving another beating. What good would it have done to tell Mr. Pugnacious the truth? His violent attitudes and actions were probably the source of Johnnie's problems. It seemed to Ms. Jones that everyone was better off because of her lie. Johnnie had not been beaten, and she had not had to confront a violent and drunken father. Surely she had been right to lie. What else could she have done? And what could she do now to help Johnnie?

## TWO WAYS TO THINK ABOUT ETHICS

Was Ms. Jones right in lying to Mr. Pugnacious? Let us assume a few things. Ms. Jones was right about the facts. Mr. Pugnacious would have beaten Johnnie. Moreover, he would have given Ms. Jones a bad time had she not produced Johnnie. She did indeed avoid some undesirable consequences. Does this decide the issue? Is it acting to avoid bad consequences or produce good ones that makes an action right? Or is it always wrong to lie? Ms. Jones strongly approves of honesty and deeply resents being lied to. Should she not treat Mr. Pugnacious as she expects to be treated by others? Isn't it always wrong to lie, even for a good cause? How would we decide?

We constructed this dilemma to illustrate the features of two major types of ethical theories—those that decide the rightness or wrongness of an action in terms of its consequences and those that do not. We shall refer to these as consequentialist theories and nonconsequentialist theories, respectively. Let us consider their basic features.

## CONSEQUENTIALIST THEORIES
## AND BENEFIT MAXIMIZATION

Consequentialist ethical theories hold that the rightness or wrongness of an action is to be decided in terms of its consequences. One way to understand consequentialist theories is to see them as committed to a principle that we will call the *principle of benefit maximization.* This principle holds that, whenever we are faced with a choice, the best and most just decision is the one that results in the most good or the greatest benefit for the most people. Thus the principle of benefit maximization judges the morality of our actions by their consequences. It says that the best action is the one with the best overall results. It does not directly tell us what is to count as a benefit or a good. That requires additional reflection. It merely says that once we know what is good, the best decision is the one that maximizes good outcomes. Thus, if Ms. Jones wished to decide on the merits of lying to Mr. Pugnacious by using consequentialist reasoning, she would have to balance the benefits and harms of lying against the benefits and harms of not lying. She would then choose the course of action with the best overall consequences. She would seek to maximize the good. But what is to count as the good?

To talk about the good is to talk about those kinds of things that are intrinsically valuable. What is it that makes something worthwhile for his own sake One of the authors of this book is in the habit or going out and running a few miles over the noon hour. It is not something he greatly enjoys. Why then do it? There are several reasons. He needs the exercise, and he enjoys the company of those he runs with. But why value exercise? And why value others' company? In the first case, he is inclined to say that what he really values is health. Perhaps, in turn, health is valued because it allows him to do certain enjoyed activities such as canoeing and skiing. So running and exercise are instrumental values. They help him get what he wants and that is why he values them. Why value the company of other people? He just does, that's all. He does not run with these people because being with them is a means to some other end. He is not trying to enhance his professional opportunities or sell them something. He simply enjoys their company. Pleasant company, skiing, and canoeing, then, are the final reasons for his conduct. There is no "in order to" about doing them. They are intrinsic goods. That is, they are valued for their own sake.

A good consequentialist is not simply interested in producing any results that are intrinsically good. Consequentialists are interested in maximizing the good, that is, producing the most good. After all, it is relatively easy to produce some good results. Every gray cloud, we are told, has a silver lining. In fact, it is difficult to do something that produces no good.

But the point is to choose that action that has the best set of consequences. If noon runs are to be justified, one must not only show that they produce some desirable consequences, but that the consequences produced are better than those consequences that would result from whatever else might be done. The good must be maximized.

Consequentialist theories can differ over what they consider good. The most influential form of consequentialism, hedonism, holds that the good is pleasure or happiness. But the Westminster Catechism answers the question "What is the chief end of man?" with the response that "The chief end of man is to glorify God and to enjoy Him forever." These are two different views about what the good is.

One of the most important varieties of consequentialism is a social application of hedonism called utilitarianism. This is a view of social justice developed in its most influential form by the English philosophers Jeremy Bentham (1748–1832) and John Stuart Mill (1806–1873). Its central doctrine is that social policy ought to be determined by what produces the greatest good for the greatest number.

How do we decide what counts as the greatest good for the greatest number? The starting point is the assumption that pleasure is good and pain is bad. If we want, therefore, to decide how well off any given individual person is, we must do so by measuring and adding up that persons total of pleasure and pain and by subtracting the total of pain from the total of pleasure. The result gives us a figure that is referred to as that person's utility. Deciding how well off a given society is is a matter of summing the utility of its individual members and dividing by the number of individuals in the population (providing, of course, that such things can be measured). This figure, known as the average utility, is a measure of general social welfare.

Deciding on the merits of a particular policy is a matter of determining its effects on the average utility. Those policies that produce the highest average utility are the most just. Thinking of moral problems from this perspective has the merit of reminding us that when we are evaluating the morality of an action or policy by judging its consequences, we must consider its consequences for everyone. If Ms. Jones is seriously to decide on the morality of lying to Mr. Pugnacious, she must consider all of the consequences for everyone affected. She must ask not only how her decision will affect her and Johnnie. She must ask such hard questions as whether her reputation as an honest person will be affected and whether any loss of respect for her truthfulness might not make her a poorer teacher. The other children in her class and in the school might also be affected by what she does. Utilitarianism requires that all of the consequences for everyone's well-being be taken into account.

Utilitarians sometimes disagree about whether the principle of benefit maximization should be applied to individual actions or to moral rules. Ms. Jones might reason thus: "The problem with asking me to decide whether it is right in this particular case to lie to Mr. Pugnacious is that I really do not have a very good idea of what the actual consequences will be. Perhaps I will save Johnnie a beating. But it is also possible that Mr. Pugnacious will find out that I lied to him. Johnnie might get an even worse beating then, and Mr. Pugnacious will never trust me again. I do, however, know that in the vast majority of cases the consequences of lying are less desirable than the consequences of truthfulness. Generally, honesty is the best policy. Since I am unsure of what the consequences of lying are in this particular case, I think I should do what I know is best as a general policy."

Here Ms. Jones has decided that it is better to apply consequentialist moral arguments to general policies rather than to individual actions. We should not have to decide whether or not to lie in each case. Instead, the appropriate question is whether a policy to permit or reject lying is best. Ms. Jones argues that it is easier to know what the consequences of certain kinds of actions are in general than it is to know what the particular consequences of a particular action will be. She might also have argued that it is dangerous to have people treat every decision as a case unto itself apart from any general rules of conduct. People are weak. Without the aid of moral rules they will do what is expedient, not what is right. And how can we have laws if we have to decide each and every case apart from the rest? Perhaps, then, it is moral rules or policies, and not actions, that should be evaluated.

Before moving on to consider nonconsequentialist arguments, we should look at two problems with consequentialism. One difficulty is that consequentialism, particularly in its utilitarian form, requires us to have information that is normally difficult or impossible to attain. Consider how difficult it is to compare pleasures or pains. Does good company produce more or less pleasure than good food? Is it worse to sit on a tack or receive a cutting insult? Utilitarianism seems to require us not only to be able to answer such questions, but to quantify them. Next, it requires us not only to know all of the consequences of our actions or policies, but to be able to judge the impact of these actions and policies for the overall distribution of pleasure and pain for everyone affected. It appears that moral behavior requires an omniscience that is unavailable to most of us.

A second difficulty is that utilitarianism can produce results that seem morally abhorrent. Let us imagine that a dozen sadistic people have had the good fortune to have captured a potential victim. They are debating whether or not it would be right to spend a pleasant evening torturing their captive. One of the group argues in the following way: "We must admit that by torturing this person we will cause a certain amount of pain. But think how much pleasure we will give ourselves. And there are a dozen of us. While this person's pain may exceed the pleasure of any one of us, it surely cannot exceed the pleasure of all of us. Thus the average utility is enhanced by torturing this person. We ought to do so." Supposing these judgments about the consequences of torture are correct, do the moral conclusions follow? If one accepts utilitarianism, they seem to. Yet we suspect our moral sensitivities would rebel against such an argument. If utilitarianism can justify such actions, perhaps we should be a bit suspicious of it.

## NONCONSEQUENTIALIST THEORIES AND RESPECT FOR PERSONS

A second way to think about Ms. Jones's behavior is suggested by another thought she expressed. Ms. Jones resents being lied to. Should she not treat Mr. Pugnacious as she expects to be treated by others?

This thought expresses a common moral idea. Its most familiar version is the Golden Rule, "Do unto others as you would have others do unto you." Might this thought not have something to contribute to the understanding of the problem?

Let us try to find out what additional ideas the Golden Rule contains by looking at it in a form offered by the German philosopher Immanuel Kant (1724–1804).[2] Kant's central moral precept is called the categorical imperative. "So act that the maxim of your will could always hold at the same time as a principle establishing universal law." This rather formidable phrase involves some less formidable moral ideas that express the content of the Golden Rule well. We will try to state the point more simply.

By a maxim or a principle Kant simply means a moral rule. "Do not kill" is an example.

What does it mean to say that a moral rule should be universal? Kant proposes a test to see if the principle underlying some action can be willed to be a universal law. If you are about to apply some moral principle to someone else, are you willing that it be applied to you in the same way? If you lie, are you willing to be lied to? If you steal, are you willing to be stolen from? If you are willing to lie but not be lied to, you are not willing that the principle that guides your behavior should be treated as a universal rule of human conduct. Kant has put in a more formal way what was implicit in Ms. Jones's reflection that she should treat Mr. Pugnacious as she would wish to be treated.

---

2. Immanual Kant, *Critique of Practical Reason* (Indianapolis, IN: Bobbs-Merrill, 1956).

According to Kant, the Golden Rule requires that we act in ways that respect the equal worth of moral agents. It requires that we regard human beings as having intrinsic worth and treat them accordingly. That is why we have a duty to accord others the same kind of treatment we expect them to accord us. We shall call this idea the principle of *equal respect for persons*. The principle of equal respect involves three subsidiary ideas.

First, the principle of equal respect requires us to treat people as *ends rather than means*. That is, we may not treat them as though they were simply means to further our own goals. We must respect their goals as well. We cannot treat people as though they were things, mere objects, who are valued only insofar as they contribute to our welfare. We must consider their welfare as well.

Second, we must regard all people as *free, rational, and responsible moral agents*. This means that we must respect their freedom of choice. And we must respect the choices people make even when we do not agree with them. Moreover, it means that we must attach a high priority to enabling people to decide responsibly. It is important that people have the information and the education that will enable them to function responsibly as free moral agents.

Third, no matter how people differ, as moral agents they are of *equal value*. This does not mean that we must see people as equal insofar as their abilities or capacities are concerned. Nor does it mean that relevant differences among people cannot be recognized in deciding how to treat them. It is not, for example, a violation of equal respect to pay one person more than another because that person works harder and contributes more. That people are of equal value as moral agents means that they are entitled to the same basic rights and that their interests, though different, are of equal value. Everyone, regardless of native ability, is entitled to equal opportunity. Everyone is entitled to one vote in a democratic election, and every vote should be worth the same as every other vote. No one is entitled to act as though his or her happiness counts more than the happiness of others. As persons, everyone has equal worth.

When Ms. Jones proposes to apply the Golden Rule in deciding whether or not to lie to Mr. Pugnacious, she is not proposing to decide what to do by determining which act has the best consequence. Instead, she is trying to decide which action is most consistent with equal respect for persons. Theories that emphasize the principle of equal respect over the principle of benefit maximization are called *nonconsequentialist* theories.

Kant would wish to argue that all consequentialist positions will end up treating some persons as though they are means to the ends of others. When we seek to maximize the average happiness, are we not saying that we may trade the happiness of some for the happiness of others so long as the average happiness increases? When we do this are we not treating the happiness of those who are made less happy as a means to the happiness of others?

Thus Ms. Jones has another way to view her decision to lie to Mr. Pugnacious. She does not have to decide what action has the best consequences. She only has to decide whether her conduct conforms to the moral law—whether it can be consistently willed to be a universal rule of human conduct. She must treat Mr. Pugnacious as an end, not a means to someone else's well-being. Then she must do her duty. Ms. Jones, therefore, has a nonconsequentialist way of thinking about her behavior.

Let us consider two difficulties with this way of thinking. First, how can someone decide whether or not they are willing to have lying become a universal rule of conduct? Why is Ms. Jones unwilling to be lied to? What would we say to someone who argues that they are perfectly happy to have lying be a universal rule of conduct, that they do not care if they are lied to? Answers to such questions are soon likely to get us around to considering the undesirable consequences of lying. Lying cannot be accepted as a universal rule precisely because it has undesirable consequences. We cannot live with one another in peace if we are not usually honest. Such a turn of events poses a dilemma for nonconsequentialist theories. If they are unwilling altogether to consider the consequences of actions as relevant to their moral appraisal, it becomes hard to see how we could ever decide whether or not some moral principle could be universally willed. If, however, they are willing to talk about consequences, they will have to explain how they are different from any other consequentialist theory.

The second difficulty concerns how generally or specifically we should express the moral principle that underlies some action. Perhaps it is clear that we could not will lying to be a universal rule of conduct, but is it not equally clear that we could will lying in order to prevent the suffering of a child as a universal rule of conduct? How specific can we make our rules? If we must express them very generally, will our behavior not seem unresponsive to what may be very real and important differences in the circumstances under which we must act? If we can express them with considerable attention to circumstances, we reintroduce all of the vagueness into our choices that the categorical imperative seemed to offer hope of avoiding. Moreover, can a moral theory that makes the morality of an action depend on the generality with which it is described be reasonable? This seems an arbitrary matter for ethical judgments to depend on.

Let us summarize. Ms. Jones's assessment of her actions seems to rely on two quite different ways of thinking about ethical matters. Both seem plausible. Neither seems fully adequate. Can these views be integrated in some reasonable fashion? Can they be used as successful tools to think about the ethics of teaching? In order to address these questions, we will spend some time in the chapters that follow working through some quite real moral dilemmas that occur in teaching. We should try to see how we can look at each dilemma from the perspective of each theory. Perhaps then we can discover if there is really any objective way to address the ethical aspects of teaching.

## ETHICAL THEORIES AND THEIR USES

Shortly we will invite you to use the distinction between consequentialist and nonconsequentialist theories as part of a conceptual tool kit to analyze and reason about a range of ethical issues. We will develop and apply this distinction throughout the book. However, we want to prepare you with an interpretation of its meaning that we hope will prove helpful. Some of what we say here is developed in more detail later, but it may help you to have a sketch of the ideas now.

The first question to consider is "Aren't there other theories?" Here the answer is that there are. A few examples: In the last several decades some feminist scholars have developed what they call an ethic of care. This view makes caring central to the ethical life and sometimes describes itself as an ethic of relationships. Other scholars have argued for an ethic of virtue, and some have linked this with an ethic of community. So there are alternative views of ethics. What shall we say of them?

One thing we might say is that it is not altogether clear that these different ethical views are inconsistent with the consequentialist/nonconsequentialist framework as we understand it. Consider a few points about this.

First, we believe that any ethic needs a concept of virtue. Good actions typically flow from good character. Character concerns what we do habitually. To possess a virtue is to have a rationally ordered habit. We do not see either nonconsequentialist of consequentialist views as precluding the importance of virtue so understood.

Similarly, we take an ethic of caring to involve an account of the human good, one which makes caring relationships central. One might argue that an ethic of caring is a kind of consequentialist ethic. Perhaps one might also construct a nonconsequentialist interpretation of an ethic of caring, but we doubt that there is much point in undertaking such an exercise. Neither interpretation of an ethic of caring would capture its point.

While we do not talk much about caring in this book, we do not dispute its importance to a good life or to good education. But our focus in this book is more with concepts that are part of a view of justice. Concepts such as intellectual liberty, equality of opportunity, and due process are (in a sense) part of an ethic of relationship for people who must relate to one another in public institutions such as schools. People rarely work well with those who treat them unfairly. Injustice undermines relationships.

The idea of an ethic of care appeared on the scene largely due to criticism of Lawrence Kohlberg's theory of moral development. Because Kohlberg's ethic was an ethic of justice, the literature often viewed an ethic of care and an ethic of justice as competitors. We think, however, that understanding justice and caring as competing visions of the moral life is a mistake. To claim otherwise is to mistake a part of the ethical life for the whole. But in this book, we are not concerned to develop a full picture of the ethical life. We are concerned to characterize a set of concepts that are important to our public life in public schools.

We also think it is a mistake to view consequentialist and nonconsequentialist ethics as competitors. We tend to see most abstract ethical theories as resulting from noticing something important about the ethical life and over generalizing it. Abstract ethical theories are illuminating because they contain accounts of important ideas, but they can distort ethical reflection if we try to make them do work to which they are not well suited.

In many cases people make good ethical decisions without the need of abstract philosophical theory. We know that it is wrong to lie or commit murder. We do not need philosophers or philosophical theories to tell us this. Nor do we need to be able to show that our moral views can be derived from some abstract philosophical theory in order to justify them. In fact, justification often proceeds in the opposite direction. We justify a moral theory by showing that it can explain our deeper moral convictions about more concrete matters.

What is the value of abstract moral theories? We think that their value is shown in enabling us to understand and think clearly about what is at stake in hard cases. Ms. Jones has a hard case. It is not a hard case because she can think about it in consequentialist and nonconsequentialist ways. It is hard because she has some reason to think that lying will produce a better outcome than telling the truth, but she is also dubious about whether this is sufficient to justify lying. The tension between what has the best consequences and what we should do as a matter of principle is a familiar one. It is captured by such familiar maxims as "The ends don't justify the means." The distinction between consequentialist and nonconsequentialist ethics helps to make that tension clearer. The distinction did not create Ms. Jones's dilemma, but it will help her to understand it better.

What the distinction between consequentialist and nonconsequentialist theories does is to enable us to ask good questions about hard cases. These different questions permit us to be clearer concerning what is at stake. When we reason about a case from a consequentialist perspective we must ask ourselves questions such as "What are the benefits we are aiming at?" "Are these benefits genuinely worthwhile?" "Are there unintended consequences we should consider?" "Whom do we intend to benefit? Are there others who are affected?" When we reason about hard cases from a nonconsequentialist perspective, we should ask questions such as "Are we being consistent?" "How would we feel were we to be treated in this way?" "Are we respecting those with whom we are interacting?" "Are the benefits distributed fairly?" "Are we treating people as ends rather than means?"

All of these questions are worth asking. We should also ask questions that are suggested by other theories. "How will our actions effect relationships?" "How will our actions affect our communities?" "Since in making a choice are we shaping our own character, do we wish to become the kind of person we may become if we make this kind of choice often?"

Thus we think of consequentialism and nonconsequentialism (as well as other theories) as tools to be employed in interrogating ethical dilemmas and hard cases. We do not see them as alternative theories among which we must choose. We have chosen to emphasize consequentialist and nonconsequentialist views because these views have an honored pedigree in philosophy and because they are very much with us still.

We have also used them because they are particularly useful in illuminating ethical concepts that are part of what might be called the civic ethic. Concepts such as just punishment, intellectual and religious liberty, and equality of opportunity are a part of our civic heritage, and they are central to ethical schools. They are not, however, all that there is to be said about ethical matters in schools. But one cannot do everything in a brief book.

How does being able to ask good questions about hard cases help us to decide what to do? There is no simple answer to this. After all a hard case is hard because it requires a choice between conflicting principles or conflicting goods. Sometimes when we ask the right questions about a hard case and we get clearer about what is at stake, we will find that our dilemma has dissolved. It only seemed to be a hard case. Sometimes we may find that all we have done is to make the dilemma sharper. What then?

One thing to notice about hard cases is that while it is usually true that some choices are better than others; it is not always the case that there is one uniquely right response. We may find that we have a conflict between competing principles and goods and that our achieving a better understanding of our possible choices helps eliminate some possibilities, but no one choice emerges as a clear winner. What then?

The best response we can give is that one has to rely on one's judgment and that sometimes you and other reasonable people will disagree and there will not be any obvious or easy way to persuade one another. We claim that objective ethical argument is possible, but we do not claim that ethics is an exact science. We do the best we can. We do not ask more of ethical reasoning than it can provide.

We also think it important that you not approach ethics as a kind of deduction of rules of conduct from first principles. Ethics is not like geometry. Ethical reasoning often begins with our intuitions about what is right or wrong. We try to formulate principles that explain how we feel. We test these principles by asking how they would apply in other kinds of cases. Sometime we find that we must alter our principles. Sometimes our principles will alter our initial intuitions. The process is not unidirectional. It is dialectical.

What we are trying to achieve in ethical reasoning is a provisional reflective equilibrium between our principles and our ethical intuitions. We have achieved a provisional conclusion when, all things considered, we have achieved a stable balance among a range of considerations.

We invite you to try out your own analyses and use of these theoretical perspectives on the following cases.

## ADDITIONAL CASES

### Truth or Consequences

Bayview High School, a racially mixed city school, enjoys the reputation of being relatively free from disciplinary problems. The administration is proud of the school and attributes this distinction to faculty cooperation and a system of communication that alerts the staff to potentially dangerous situations.

Recently, there have been some disturbances in the student body, and there have been some fights instigated by racial epithets. The staff, aware of these hostilities, was alerted to watch for weapons and other dangerous articles in the possession of students.

One Monday at lunch, Ms. Miller announced in the staff dining room that her wallet had been taken from her purse that morning. Twenty dollars was missing.

After classes ended that afternoon, Chico Diaz walked into the school store before leaving the building. He carefully took off his sweatshirt, checked the pockets, and placed it on a desk. He proceeded to the counter to purchase some school tee-shirts, notebooks, and pen sets. He produced a twenty-dollar bill as payment. Ms. Burner, the teacher in charge of the school store, noticed the bill, and she became suspicious. She went to the desk and looked in the pocket of Chico's sweatshirt, thinking that Ms. Miller's wallet might be there. What she discovered instead was a large switchblade knife. She placed the sweatshirt back in its original position and immediately summoned Mr. Marconi, the dean of discipline.

Mr. Marconi requested that Chico empty his pockets. When Chico did what was asked, the knife was discovered. Mr. Marconi, a strict disciplinarian, called in the principal, Mr. Lopez. Chico was informed that he was to leave the building immediately and consider himself suspended, pending a hearing on the matter the next morning with representatives of the school board.

Before the staff left the school, Ms. Burner was asked to visit Mr. Lopez in his office, and he asked her to be a party in the suspension hearing. Ms. Burner explained to Mr. Lopez that she had searched Chico's sweatshirt because she had been suspicious about another matter, not the knife. The knife had not been in sight. Mr. Lopez asked if Chico had seen her do this. When she replied that he had not, he said, "Good. At the hearing tomorrow you say that you saw the knife hanging from his pocket. That will satisfy the board."

There is a saying that the Bill of Rights does not stop at the schoolhouse door. In this case, it does not seem that Chico will receive due process, and Ms. Burner's search of his sweatshirt might not be legal. Chico does possess certain rights to privacy, as would any other citizen, and his treatment seems to be unfair. However, teachers and administrators have a responsibility to preserve the peace of the school and protect the other students. In this sense, an appeal to the general welfare is an attempt to justify the treatment that Chico is receiving. After all, he did have a knife.

Ms. Burner feels a bit guilty about the whole affair. She wonders if her search of Chico's clothing was the right thing to do. Now she is being asked by her superior to lie during the hearing. Chico has never been a very bad student, and she is afraid that the suspension is unwarranted and may have unforeseen consequences. What would you do if you were Ms. Burner?

*Some Questions*

1. Would you lie in this case if you were Ms. Burner? Why or why not? How is lying in this case similar and different from Ms. Jones's lie to Mr. Pugnacious?
2. Do both a consequentialist and a nonconsequentialist analysis of this case. Which seems more justified?
3. Which principle, benefit maximization or respect for persons, seems more important here? Why?

## The Electrician

The consolidated high school of East Fork serves a large, sparsely populated area and draws students from as much as 20 miles away. Teachers often serve in more than one capacity to flesh out the functions of full staffing in the small school. Henry Trueblood teaches English, but he also assists in coaching football and track. Two years ago, when the full-time guidance counselor left, the principal asked Henry to take up some of that load in exchange for teaching one less section of composition. Henry quickly agreed. Besides having fewer poorly written themes to grade, he found that he rather liked helping students apply for college or land jobs in the local area. It gave him a different kind of satisfaction as a teacher—at least it had until now.

He had to make a tough decision about a reference. Tim Mulberry had never been a very good student. In fact, it was touch and go whether or not he would meet the minimum requirements for graduation next month. Tim was probably of average intelligence, but he never really applied himself at school. Henry now had him as a student in senior English. Tim handed in work late or not at all; he was sloppy and slapdash with his writing and at times Henry could not believe English was his first and only language. He had heard from other teachers that this was just Tim.

Still, Tim had had a hard life. More often unemployed than not, his father was in and out of the local jail for drunkenness and wife beating. His mother supported the family with a poorly paying job at the dime store and worked nights as a waitress. Tim received very little support and encouragement at home. He often got into trouble at school. Notes and calls to his home had little effect. Tim was within a whisker of failing English.

So Henry was surprised and delighted to find a letter on his counselor's desk informing him that Tim had applied to the union to become an apprentice electrician. Tim seemed to have some get-up-and-go after all. The letter asked for confirmation that Tim would graduate in June and a reference regarding his suitability for becoming an electrician.

Henry had a big problem. This might be Tim's only chance to learn a trade and lead a productive life. If he failed in his first attempt outside of school to make a go of things, he might give up altogether and join his father in the unemployment line. On the other hand, if Henry stretched the truth a bit, he might be obliged to pass Tim in English next month whether Tim deserved it or not. Moreover, Tim's work habits hardly seemed suitable to a trade in which mistakes could cause fire or shock in the homes and businesses of trusting clients. What should he do?

*Some Questions*

1. If you were Henry, what would you say in your response to the request of the electricians' union for a reference? Would you lie about Tim's work habits? If you just did not tell the union what you knew about Tim's undependability and carelessness, would that be untruthful? How would you treat the graduation issue?
2. Recommendations are requested all the time from employment agencies, organizations, prospective employers, and colleges. Should the records of students and opinions of teachers and counselors be made

available to anyone who asks? The presumption of truth telling is essential to this process. Is that a realistic assumption?

3.  How do the principles of benefit maximization and respect for persons apply in this case?

## FOR FURTHER INQUIRY

Bok, Sissela. *Lying: Moral Choice in Public and Private Life.* New York: Vintage, 1979.
    Addresses the possible justifications and consequences of withholding the truth.

Gilligan, Carol. *In a Different Voice.* Cambridge, MA: Harvard University Press, 1982.
    A critique of the view of Lawrence Kohlberg claiming that they ignore the importance of caring and relationships in ethics.

Kant, Immanuel. *Critique of Practical Reason,* trans. Lewis W. Beck. Indianapolis, IN: Bobbs-Merrill, 1956.
    The classical statement and defense of a nonconsequentialist ethical position. Hard reading, but worthwhile.

Kohlberg, Lawrence. "From Is to Ought: How to Commit the Naturalistic Fallacy and Get Away with It in the Study of Moral Development." In *Cognitive Development and Epistemology.* New York: Academic Press, 1971.
    This is an excellent statement of Lawrence Kohlberg's theory of moral development.

MacIntyre, Alasdair. *After Virtue.* South Bend, IN: University of Notre Dame Press, 1982.
    A recent influential statement of a communitarian and virtue ethic.

Mill, John Stuart. *Utilitarianism.* Reprinted in *The Utilitarian.* New York: Doubleday, 1961.
    An excellent and brief statement of utilitarianism.

NEA. "Code of Ethics of the Education Profession." National Education Association, http://www.nea.org/aboutnea/code.html
    The online text of the NEA Code along with other resources for teachers.

Noddings, Nel. *The Challenge to Care in Schools: An Alternative Approach to Education.* New York: Teachers College Press, 1992.
    A discussion of the ethic of care in the context of schooling.

Strike, Kenneth A. "Justice, Caring, and Universality: In Defense of Moral Pluralism." In *Justice and Caring: The Search for Common Ground in Education,* edited by Michael Katz, Nel Noddings and Kenneth Strike, 21–36. New York: Teachers College Press, 1999.
    A discussion of the justice/caring debate.

Strike, Kenneth A. "The Ethics of Teaching." In *A Companion to the Philosophy of Education,* edited by Randall Curren, 509–24. Oxford: Blackwell, 2003.
    A discussion of how we should think about the ethics of teaching.

# Chapter 2

# Punishment and
# Due Process

The NEA Code of Ethics contains the following statements:

> In fulfillment of the obligation to the student, the educator...
> 4. Shall make reasonable effort to protect the student from conditions harmful to learning or to health and safety.
> 5. Shall not intentionally expose the student to embarrassment or disparagement.

These precepts raise the issue of punishment. Punishment is often seen as a means of maintaining proper order and thus of eliminating conditions incompatible with learning and with a safe environment. Punishment can also subject the student to a risk of embarrassment or disparagement. What kinds of moral concepts are needed to discuss punishment intelligently?

## A CASE TO CONSIDER

Mr. Fuse is the chemistry teacher at Middletown High. One day, while he was supervising a rather innocuous lab session, he was asked to report to the office to take an emergency call about one of his children. Noting that there was no possible danger in the experiment being conducted and that any really dangerous materials were locked up, he told his class to keep working and went off to take his call.

Mr. Fuse remembered two things about that day. The first was how relieved he was to find out that the "emergency" really was not one. The second was how panicked he became when he heard the explosion in the chemistry lab.

Running back as fast as he could, he entered the room to find it filled with smoke. His first concern was to discover if anyone was hurt.

No one was. Indeed, the students appeared to find it quite amusing. Whoever had set the explosion had set if off in a formidable metal wastebasket. There was little chance of anyone's having been hurt.

Mr. Fuse next noticed that one of the locked cabinets was open. He was certain that he had locked it. Someone, he concluded, had a key or was able to pick the lock.

Mr. Fuse considered the situation to be very serious. The student who had set off the blast may have had only the foggiest idea of what he or she was doing. The student might have erred and blown up half the school. Moreover, now someone had access to his supplies. There were things in those cabinets that, if mishandled, could be lethal. He thus began to question the class to find out who was responsible. He had no luck. It became apparent that many students had been doing their work and did not know who had done it. What annoyed Mr. Fuse, however, was that many students obviously did know who had done it. None of them were willing to point out the guilty person.

Mr. Fuse decided to punish the entire class. He gave them detention for a month and assigned them a thirty-page paper on the chemistry of explosions. Anyone who failed to do the assignment would fail chemistry. Detention, Mr. Fuse said, would be canceled when he found out who did it.

The next morning, Mr. Fuse found an anonymous note on his desk accusing a student named Alex of setting the blast. That made sense. Alex was bright enough to know what to do. Moreover, Alex was the school's most notable practical joker. Alex's popularity or his size, strength, and aggressiveness easily explained why no one would turn him in. The real clincher, however, was that Alex's father was a locksmith. All the pieces fit.

The only problem was that Alex refused to admit his guilt when confronted with the charge. That bothered Mr. Fuse a lot. He had only circumstantial evidence, and that was none too conclusive. Nevertheless, Mr. Fuse decided to punish Alex. The next day he announced that since the guilty person had been apprehended, he was lifting the class detention. Alex, however, was given detention for the rest of the year and a failing grade in chemistry. Mr. Fuse fully intended to make an example of him. He was responsible for the safety of his students. At all costs he had to make him understand that setting explosions was a serious matter. Being severe with Alex was a small price to pay for preventing a potentially terrible incident. No student hereafter would be able to think of getting into the chemistry supplies or setting an explosion as a harmless prank.

Has Mr. Fuse behaved fairly or justly? Let us consider first a brief argument for each side.

We may defend Mr. Fuse by noting that his first responsibility is to ensure the safety of his class. A dangerous situation has arisen. Someone has access to his supplies and seems willing to use this access to play practical jokes. Moreover, Mr. Fuse's class seems not to appreciate the seriousness of the matter. They regard it as humorous. Thus, it is quite reasonable to suppose that if something is not done there will be further incidents. Since the chemistry supplies contain materials that if mishandled can be life threatening, Mr. Fuse must take whatever action necessary to guarantee the security of his supplies and the safety of his students. His actions have very likely done that. At least he has demonstrated how seriously he views the incident and has shown his willingness to deal severely with offenders.

On the other hand, Mr. Fuse can be accused of dealing unfairly with both Alex and the entire class. Alex has been treated unfairly by being punished even though Mr. Fuse is not at all sure that he is guilty. Also, the punishment given to Alex seems inappropriate to the offense. Mr. Fuse has failed Alex in chemistry. Course grades, however, are normally based on knowledge of subject matter. Anyone who sees Alex's transcript will conclude that he failed to learn chemistry, not that he is being punished. Finally, Mr. Fuse punished some people he knows are not guilty to deter others from getting into the chemistry supplies. He punished the entire class even though he knew that most of the students had not been guilty and that many of them did not know who the guilty person was. Thus, Mr. Fuse can be accused of having done several unfair things. Before we begin to explore these issues in some depth, it may be useful to highlight several ideas regarding the use of punishment in schools. We offer the following imaginary dispute.

## DISPUTE

A:  As a teacher, I do not believe in punishment. It may be necessary in the world at large, but in school it serves no educational purpose.

B:  But of course it does! Education cannot go on without order and peace in a classroom of learners. Could you imagine a school or classroom without any rules to govern behavior? Of course not! And if there are rules, there are sure to be infractions of them now and then. And if there are infractions, there must be provision for punishment or else there is no reason for students to obey the rules. Right?

A:  Then you think that fear of punishment deters students from breaking rules. But obviously that is not true. Rules get broken no matter how harsh the punishment, and there is a limit to the harshness we can impose. Besides, fear may not be the best educational tool for teaching students to act properly. When fear of punishment does not deter, what is the good of punishing a student?

B:  Well, you have to punish transgressors to give them their due. Justice demands it, doesn't it? I mean, if you knowingly act wrongly, you have to accept the consequences. It's an important lesson for students to learn about life and that is the educational purpose of punishment: to learn about justice.

A: But is it just to punish a whole class for the actions of only one or just a few members of the class? Teachers seem to do that all the time! Wouldn't it be more instructive to help students see that there are different reasons for following the rules and that some are better, more just than others? Fear of punishment is not as good a moral reason for acting properly as is respect for rules and laws or the sense of duty to do what society requires of its members. School rules are not made to underwrite punishment, but are necessary to maintain conditions appropriate to learning and safety, and students should learn that.

B: That may be true for some rules, but what do school dress codes and the like have to do with safety or learning or justice? I mean, are all school rules really essential to education or are some just forced on the young arbitrarily by an older generation? And what about the unjust application of rules?

How can students learn about justice when so often the innocent are punished by presumably just teachers and administrators who don't even give them a chance to defend themselves? There is no court of appeal, no jury system, no chance to challenge authority and present evidence in one's defense. Punishment is meted out directly and arbitrarily. Authority is not to be questioned. Justice is whatever those in power decree and decide.

A: You sound like you are on my side now. See how dysfunctional and uneducational punishment can be in school? As I said at the beginning, punishment serves no educational purpose that cannot better be served in more humane ways. Let's scrap punishment and teach good ethical reasons for right action.

B: But what do you do with the rule breakers? We really are back at the beginning!

## CONCEPTS

One of the central ideas important in discussing punishment in schools and in the case of Mr. Fuse and Alex is that of due process. The general idea of due process is that people are entitled to procedures that ensure that decisions made about them are not arbitrary or capricious. Decisions are made arbitrarily when they are made without evidence. To find someone guilty of an offense without having sufficient evidence to ensure guilt is to behave arbitrarily. Decisions are made capriciously when they are made unsystematically or are based on irrelevant grounds. A judge who gives out significantly different sentences to people guilty of the same offense or who bases sentences on factors such as hair color behaves capriciously.

In order to prevent arbitrary or capricious judgments, free societies often insist that people who make decisions about others follow certain procedures that require them to confront available evidence and to base their decisions on it. Such procedures are commonly associated with criminal courts, but they are important wherever one person has the power of decision over another. A teacher who fails to read assignments carefully when grading, who gives tests that fail to measure accurately what the student can reasonably be expected to learn, or who assigns grades for reasons unrelated to learning violates important rules of due process.

In this case, Mr. Fuse can be accused of not following the kinds of procedures that are important in establishing guilt. He failed to give Alex a chance to defend himself, and he failed to tell Alex why he believed him to be guilty so that he could defend himself knowledgeably. Moreover, he relied on an anonymous note, having no idea of the reliability of its author. Certainly Alex had no opportunity to confront the person who accused him. Finally, Mr. Fuse failed to investigate the matter thoroughly. He did not attempt to discover who wrote the note; nor did he question other students to see if he could learn more about the incident. Instead, he convicted and punished Alex on weak circumstantial evidence.

Mr. Fuse also gave Alex a punishment that was inappropriate to the offense. First, the punishment was not chosen because its severity seemed appropriate to the severity of the offense. Instead, the punishment was chosen for its deterrent effects. Mr. Fuse did not ask himself what kind of punishment Alex deserved to get. He asked himself what sort of punishment would deter other students from doing something similar. Second, Mr. Fuse used a grade as a punishment. Arguably, grades are only properly granted on the basis of achievement. They are not suitable tools for punishment.

The final problem is that Mr. Fuse has punished the innocent. In this case, in order to deter future incidents, he gave an assignment and detention to the entire class despite the fact that he knew that some students were guilty neither of setting the explosion nor of withholding information about who had. He has been willing to punish some whom he knows are innocent to impress on all the seriousness of the incident and to make sure that the guilty are also punished.

Can Mr. Fuse defend himself against these charges? He might argue that some of his actions were regrettable, but necessary. He would have liked to have spent a few days investigating the matter more thoroughly in order to be sure that Alex was guilty, but it was important to act immediately before something else happened and while the incident was still fresh enough in the students' minds to allow them to profit from the example made of Alex. It seemed likely that Alex was guilty, and it was worth the risk of punishing someone who was innocent to prevent the possibility of a real disaster.

A similar argument might be given for the other objections. Perhaps a grade is not the best punishment, and perhaps there are difficulties in punishing the entire class; nevertheless, these actions were necessary to impress on the class that explosions were not a laughing matter. It was a successful lesson given in potentially dangerous circumstances. Mr. Fuse was merely taking seriously his responsibility toward the safety of his students. How could he forgive himself if his sense of fairness resulted in a serious accident, perhaps even the death of one of his students?

## ANALYSIS

Let us look at these arguments from a consequentialist perspective. A consequentialist can be expected to have a reasonable regard for the idea of due process. After all, reasonable, conscientiously made decisions are far more likely to have desirable consequences than arbitrary and capricious ones. At the same time, a consequentialist is unlikely to treat rules of due process as absolute. Like any rules, they will produce different consequences when applied in different contexts. There will be cases when they ought to be laid aside. When following such rules produces potential danger or high levels of inefficiency, they should be modified or set aside. It is possible to place such high demands on public servants to justify their decisions that they cannot act. And it is possible to have such elaborate protections for the accused that it becomes difficult to convict even the guilty. The kinds of due process we provide must be determined by weighing the consequences of possible erroneous or unfair decisions against the consequences of failing to act decisively when there is a need.

If we are to decide about the kinds of due process to provide in cases of punishment, we must have some idea of what the desirable consequences of punishment are. Consequentialists have made three suggestions. Punishment may deter the individual punished or others from doing the same thing; punishment may help rehabilitate the guilty party; and punishment may separate a potentially dangerous person from society. In this case, we need not be concerned with the third of these ideas. No one has suggested suspending Alex from school; thus the issue is not raised. Nor was Mr. Fuse particularly interested in reforming Alex. The point of his actions was to deter future incidents. Is this a good reason for Mr. Fuse's behavior?

Here both of the earlier objections brought to bear against consequentialist arguments have some force. How does Mr. Fuse know what the consequences of his actions will be? Surely there are other stories to be told than his. If Alex is not guilty, the real guilty party may be emboldened to try again. Others, seeing that the probability of getting caught is small, may help. Some members of the class, seeing that Alex has been treated unfairly, may become alienated from school and become more prone to vandalism. This may occur even if Alex is guilty. Alex may become sufficiently embittered to do something unpleasant. In fact, the consequences of Mr. Fuse's actions are highly speculative and virtually unknowable. How can we determine whether he has acted correctly if we must know the consequences of his treatment of Alex and compare them to the consequences of treating Alex differently?

Even worse, it appears that consequentialist arguments have difficulty in giving a convincing reason why it is right to punish the guilty and not the innocent. In this case, it is entirely possible that punishing Alex will have deterring effects whether or not Alex happens to be guilty. If we are to judge punishment entirely by its consequences, why should we care if Alex is guilty so long as punishing him deters others from similar behavior? A possible response to this is that punishment is unlikely to deter people if they do not believe that the probability that they will be punished is related to their guilt. But this response misses the point. What it requires is not that the guilty be punished, but that it be believed that the guilty are being punished. What seems to be needed is some reason to believe that it is inherently right to punish the guilty and not the innocent.

A similar difficulty results if we consider the nature of the punishment. If the point of punishment is to deter improper behavior, then what is important about punishment is that it actually deter. Unfortunately this does not require punishment to fit the crime. It may well be that a severe punishment is required in order to deter minor offenses. Perhaps this is not always the case or even often the case, but again this misses the point. Consequentialism provides no reason why the punishment must fit the crime, and it can occasionally provide reasons why it should not.

Perhaps, then, we should ask how punishment might be thought of from a nonconsequentialist perspective.

The most common nonconsequentialist response is to hold that the point of punishment is to balance the scales of justice, "an eye for an eye." Evil deeds are to be set right by inflicting pain on those who do them. Justice demands that evil be punished. Thus punishment is not intended primarily to deter further evil (although a nonconsequentialist may regard this as an added benefit); it is designed to provide retribution.

Viewing punishment as retribution explains why it is right to punish the guilty and not the innocent. Obviously, if the guilty person has not been punished, retribution has not been received. Similarly, the retribution theory explains why the punishment must fit the crime. If the retribution exceeds the evil, the scales of justice have not been balanced. The importance of punishing the guilty and of fitting the punishment to the offense explains the importance of due process. It is, after all, the provision of due process that permits us to be sure that we are in fact punishing the guilty in appropriate ways.

While it might seem odd to hold that this view of punishment is consistent with the principle of respect for persons, in fact it may be. We can only punish people who have done something morally wrong if we regard them as free moral agents who are responsible for their actions. Thus punishment can be seen as a way of regarding people as moral agents and as respecting their freedom to choose. If we see punishment as a way of people's accepting responsibility and retiring a debt of guilt, then we can also see it as a way of treating people as ends rather than means. Finally, it seems possible that guilty people might be willing to agree that morally wrong acts should be punished even when they are the objects of the punishment. Thus this view of punishment could meet the nonconsequentialist's test of universality.

From this analysis it would seem that Mr. Fuse will be able to make a better case for himself if he relies on consequentialist arguments. Perhaps the consequentialist case on his behalf is not foolproof, but the nonconsequentialist case that we have argued against him seems strong. Before we accept this conclusion, however, we should look at potential problems with the nonconsequentialist position.

Perhaps the weakest point in the retribution theory of punishment is the suggestion that the universe somehow requires that evildoers be punished with a compensating quantity of pain. Why should we believe this? The point can be put more forcefully. The retribution theory seems to require that we respond to one evil event by adding a second. How is the universe improved by adding an additional piece of suffering to it? If we are to punish evildoers, ought we not to expect some good to result? Otherwise, does not punishment merely add gratuitously to the pain in the world?

We might formulate this point in the nonconsequentialist's own value system. The underlying moral demand of nonconsequentialist views is that one recognize the value of persons as ends in themselves by showing them respect. How does it show respect for the worth of persons to cause them pain even when no good results? It is hard to see how inflicting pain on the guilty per se shows respect for their value as persons.

This argument provides another way of making the point that nonconsequentialist arguments tend eventually to display an interest in the consequences of actions in order to determine if they are ethical. It seems

that it is difficult to decide whether or not to punish a guilty person without knowing if some good will result.

Rule vs. Act Consequentialism

## REFLECTIONS ON METHOD

Where does this leave us? We are not going to attempt to resolve either the
difficulties of the case or the underlying philosophical arguments. These
require long and serious thought. Before moving on to another issue, however, we would like to make a few observations about some of the conclusions to which we think these discussions point.

One conclusion that seems plausible at this point is that neither a pure
consequentialist nor a pure nonconsequentialist view is likely to be successful. Consequentialist views seem capable of justifying immoral conduct in order to produce good consequences. Nonconsequentialist views
seem to need to take consequences into account in order to be fully adequate. Perhaps, then, we need to see if there is any way to combine their
best features.

Regarding the possibility of having objective ethical knowledge, there
would seem to be good news and bad news. On one hand, we do seem to
be able to conduct meaningful ethical arguments. It does seem possible to
produce considerations that count for and against some ethical proposition. That at least suggests that ethical claims are not simply matters of
taste. It is hard to know how to begin to have an argument about a matter
that is entirely a matter of personal preference.

On the other hand, we have not been particularly successful in re-
solving any of the disputes we have raised. If we are going to succeed in
showing that ethics can be an objective matter, we will have to show more
than that such matters can be discussed. We will have to show that they
can be rationally resolved.

So that the reader does not become too quickly discouraged, we would
like to note that one reason that the case is difficult to resolve is that we have
purposefully made it as morally ambiguous as possible. Its ambiguity
makes it interesting and a good teaching tool. Its difficulty does not show
that moral issues cannot be resolved or that thinking about ethics never gets
us anywhere. Had we constructed a case in which Mr. Fuse had punished
an innocent person, but which lacked some of the complexities of the current case, we believe that almost everyone would agree he had behaved
unjustly. And we think that this conclusion could be successfully argued in
both consequentialist and nonconsequentialist ways. We also believe that
we could use the material in the discussion to show you that certain kinds
of common practices in schools (such as disciplinary practices that punish

an entire class because of the behavior of a few) are morally wrong. This case and many of the others we will give you are genuinely hard cases that involve conflicts between important moral principles. But not all cases are hard cases. Indeed, in our day-to-day lives, most of them are not. Perhaps many of our real moral dilemmas can be resolved by moral reflection.

We should add that many of the arguments presented have involved an appeal not only to reason, but also to an intuitive sense of the right thing to do. It seems intuitively wrong to punish an innocent person even if doing so produces good consequences. It seems intuitively wrong to punish a guilty person when there is no good to achieve thereby. These intuitions have been used as a kind of data against which ethical theories are tested.

Is this a legitimate strategy? It would seem important in answering this question to know what the source of our ethical intuitions is. Do we have some innate sense of justice that we must try to articulate fully?

Do we know what is right when we cannot formulate the moral principle behind it in the same way that we know the proper use of a word even though we cannot define it? Perhaps we are blessed with insight into the nature of right conduct. Or perhaps our moral intuitions are formed by our training—the voice of our culture, so to speak, whispering in our ear.

These thoughts do not yet provide much assistance in our inquiry. Perhaps, however, they will be worth keeping in mind as we move on to issues of intellectual freedom. Before going on, you and your class might want to consider other cases of punishment and due process to get another perspective on this sensitive area.

## ADDITIONAL CASES

### A Graduating Senior

Nancy Smith is a graduating senior at The Day School, a well-established private school somewhere in the Northeast. She comes from a wealthy family and has just been admitted to an Ivy League college. Nancy is probably a nice girl deep down, but parental pressure has turned her into a sneaky and conniving student. Throughout her high-school career her teachers have complained that she is dishonest and manipulative. None of them were willing to give her an enthusiastic college recommendation, but she made the college she wanted anyway. She has complained about final grades on several occasions and has even questioned teachers' judgment.

Nancy took an elective English course in her last semester for which she did little work. Her teacher, Diane Jacobs, noted that Nancy often missed class but was excused by her mother for various reasons. Ms. Jacobs suspects that Nancy did not read the one book central to the course, *Pride and Prejudice*. However, Nancy submitted a final essay, comparing *Pride and Prejudice* to Dante's *Inferno*, that, according to every member of the English department, could have been submitted with pride in a graduate seminar. Ms. Jacobs is convinced that Nancy did not write the paper. Either she was given a great deal of help, or she plagiarized some of the information, or she plagiarized all of it. In any event, the entire English department is convinced that Nancy could not have written the paper. Many of them have taught her in other courses; some of them have accused her of plagiarism in the past. Nancy's paper contained many footnotes to *Pride and Prejudice* and the *Inferno*, but there are no references in it to any outside sources.

Ms. Jacobs had already met with Nancy several times. On one occasion Nancy was given a test on her own paper. She was asked to explain some of the statements made in the paper; she was also asked some simple factual questions about *Pride and Prejudice*. Nancy did quite poorly on these questions, reconfirming Ms. Jacobs's suspicions that Nancy neither read the book nor wrote the paper. More alarming, perhaps, was the indication from the test that Nancy had not read the *Inferno* either. Despite several opportunities to reveal her sources, Nancy has only mentioned some discussions with her sister's fiancé, a college student. She seems unwilling to concede that she had any help whatsoever.

Ms. Jacobs and the English department have brought the matter to the attention of the headmaster, Mr. Fitzgerald. They have presented the facts clearly and have demanded action on his part. They have recommended that Nancy not be allowed to graduate but that she be allowed to make up the course in the summer and, upon its successful completion, be granted late graduation. Mr. Fitzgerald has reviewed the case, remembering that Nancy has been a student at The Day School for thirteen years. He has also reminded himself that Mrs. Smith was just elected to the Board of Trustees. He does not need to be reminded that the Smiths are very wealthy people who might be making major future contributions to the school. Mr. Fitzgerald does not want to antagonize the Smiths if he can help it, but he does not want to alienate his teachers either. What should he do?

*Some Questions*

1. Do you think due process was followed in this case?
2. Do you think the punishment recommended fits the crime? Presumably other students have heard about Nancy's case. Should this have a bearing on Mr. Fitzgerald's decision?
3. Inevitably, in the real world, people of money and influence get special consideration. Although this is not fair, it might result in benefit maxi-

mization for an entire school, as in this case. Realistically, do you think such considerations are ethically warranted? Can you invent a case in which this point of view is persuasive? On what grounds might you object to such considerations even in the most persuasive case?

## Bang! Zero Tolerance

It was a gun—a real gun. James had brought a gun to school. Ms. Hesston couldn't believe it. James was a shy kid who seemed to get along with everyone. It was hard to imagine him as a gang member or a drug dealer. It was hard to imagine him as anything other than a nice fourth-grade boy. What did he want with a gun? But there it was. She had seen the bulge under his jacket, which he refused to take off. She had asked him what he had under his coat. James was not good at weapons concealment. He had taken it out and put it on her desk. And it was a real gun. He had taken it from his father's dresser drawer.

Thank God it wasn't loaded! James had not intended to shoot anyone. In fact, he had carefully removed all the bullets before he brought the gun to school. But apparently he had intended to threaten someone. She got the story out of him bit by bit. Every day after school, two bigger boys met James and demanded his money. If he refused, they took it anyway. If he didn't have any money, they punched him and shoved him around. James only had his lunch money to bring to school. In order to have something to give them, he had stopped eating lunch. "Why didn't you tell me about this, James?" Ms. Hesston asked. "Why didn't you tell your parents?" James just shrugged. "I didn't think you would be able to do anything," he said. "If you tried to protect me, they would get me later and hurt me worse. Can you protect me all the time? Are you going to put them in jail?" His point was well taken. The school didn't manage bullying well. Ms. Hesston suspected that the point of the gun wasn't really to threaten the bullies. It was to get the school to take his problem seriously. Perhaps he would succeed in this.

But James didn't know about the school district's zero tolerance policy. Neither Ms. Hesston nor the school's principal had any discretion about what to do with James. She would take James to the principal's office, and the principal would call the police. James would have a hearing in juvenile court. He would also be expelled and placed in an "alternative program." Ms. Hesston didn't know whether juvenile court had some discretion about what happened to James, but the school had no choice. This is what zero tolerance means—no discretion, no taking circumstances into account. There would not be a discussion with James's parents about what was best for him, and there would not be a discussion about the educational consequences of what was decided. Zero tolerance was mandated by state law pursuant to requirements of federal legislation. James was going to have a tough time.

Unless she could handle it quietly by herself or she could try to persuade the principal to ignore the matter for James's sake. No, she couldn't do that. Ignoring the gun was illegal. If the zero tolerance policy were to be ignored, she would have to take the responsibility for it herself. Why couldn't she, the principal, and James's parents just sit down and decide what to do? Isn't that how problems like this should be solved?

*Some Questions*

1. Teachers and administrators often claim to want discretion over such matters so that they can consider mitigating circumstances and so that they can take the best interests of the child into consideration. Are these good reasons for giving them more discretion? Is this how such discretion is likely to be used?
2. Here are two arguments for zero tolerance policies:
   a. We need to send a message that drugs and guns aren't tolerated. Tough penalties and no exceptions send this message. Kids will hear it. Letting educators work things out with parents sends the message that kids can get away with drugs and guns in school.
   b. Educators are self-serving and soft-hearted. It's nice to say that they should have discretion about appropriate penalties, but it's always more convenient for them to let kids off, and educators always think kids need one more chance. We need to do the same thing with educators that we did with judges who are too soft on crime—take away their discretion and make them hand out tough penalties.

   Is either of these arguments a good argument?
3. Is it morally permissible for Ms. Hesston to violate the law to protect James?
4. Is expulsion a fair penalty for James's crime?
5. Suppose that expulsion isn't fair to James, but that tough zero tolerance policies do reduce shooting incidents and drug usage, does that justify enforcing the policies?

## FOR FURTHER INQUIRY

American Civil Liberties Union. http://www.aclu.org/studentsrights/dueprocess/index.html
   The ACLU is a civil rights organization. This link takes you to a page concerning student rights and due process.

Ezorsky, Gertrude, ed. *Philosophical Perspectives on Punishment.* Albany: State University of New York Press, 1972.
> A useful collection of essays, classical and modern, on the ethics of punishment.

Fischer, Louis, David Schimmel, and Leslie R. Stellman. *Teachers and the Law.* 6th ed. Boston: Allyn and Bacon, 2003, Chapter 12.
> A discussion of the law of due process for teachers and students.

*Goss* v. *Lopez* 419 U.S. 565 (1975). http://www.law.cornell.edu/supct/html/historics/USSC_CR_0419_0565_ZS.html ✓
> The main Supreme Court precedent on due process and student discipline. The link takes you to Cornell University's Legal Information Institute, a useful source for Supreme Court cases and other legal information.

Kirp, David. "Proceduralism and Bureaucracy." *Stanford Law Review 84* (1976): 859– 64. ✓
> A discussion of the claim that the legal protection of due process overly restricts the discretion of teachers and administrators.

Murtagh, Kevin. "Punishment." *The Internet Encyclopedia of Philosophy* (2006), ✓ http://www.iep.utm.edu/p/punishme.htm
> An excellent summary of various ethical views on punishment.

Strike, K. with Soltis, J. (1986). Who broke the fish tank? and other ethical dilemmas. *Instructor,* 95:5, 36–39. ✓
> A treatment of the ethics of group punishment.

*Chapter 3*

# Intellectual Freedom

A second group of statements in the NEA Code holds that the educator:

1.  Shall not unreasonably restrain the student from independent action in the pursuit of learning.
2.  Shall not unreasonably deny the student access to varying points of view.
3.  Shall not deliberately suppress or distort subject matter relevant to the student's progress.

Students thus are entitled to some kind of intellectual openness. Why and of what sort?

## A CASE TO CONSIDER

Mr. Lane looked at the page proofs for the article one more time. Eddie Ribald was a talented writer all right. Mr. Lane wondered how anyone with Eddie's sensitivity to words could have such a lack of sensitivity to people.

The article in question was a piece that Eddie had prepared for the *Springfield High Odyssey,* the school's literary magazine. Mr. Lane was the faculty adviser to the magazine.

Mr. Lane had to admit that Eddie's piece was marvelously written. It was so well done that Mr. Lane almost wondered if it was true. So would many students. Unfortunately, it was also so well done that no one could fail to recognize the characters. Eddie had their mannerisms and distinctive ways of speaking down so well that the fictitious names and the change of place would fool no one.

The story dealt with the seduction/rape of a high-school student named Sue Cross by a shop teacher named Alexander Wells. It spent most of the time analyzing Sue's feelings after the incident. Eddie described her anguish and despair and her drift into alcoholism with considerable feeling. Moreover, he presented Wells with some skill as a brutish clod who was incapable of caring how he hurt other people. Mr. Lane wished that he had Eddie's talent.

Nor was Eddie's story without socially redeeming value. Eddie had woven some interesting and well-developed themes about adolescent sexuality into the fabric of his story. And he had some important things to say about abortion. The story contained ideas worth considering.

Unfortunately, the similarity between the fictional Mr. Wells and the real John Waters, Springfield's physical education teacher, would be lost on no one. Nor could the similarity between Sue Cross and Beth Straight be missed. Springfield was a small school. Everyone knew everyone else.

Mr. Lane found it difficult to show much sympathy for Waters. He was a brutish clod. But it was doubtful that Waters was in the business of assaulting female students. He was not that stupid, and he did not seem to want for female companionship outside of school. Indeed, he had quite a reputation. But his penchant for humiliating the less athletic portion of the student body was well known. Less well known was his capacity for being rude to other members of the staff. Mr. Waters was something of a physical specimen who found an almost infinite number of ways to tell other men, both students and faculty, that muscles were what counted in life and that they were clearly inferior breeds.

Yes, Mr. Lane understood why Eddie would dislike Mr. Waters. He shared the feeling. Eddie was no athlete. No doubt he had come in for some painful moments at Mr. Waters's hands. Indeed, Mr. Lane suspected that that explained Eddie's story. It was very likely a piece of revenge.

His real concern was for Beth. It had taken him a while to understand why Eddie had picked her. Mr. Lane could not recall ever having met a nicer person. It was not that she was especially popular or especially attractive. It was just that she was one of the kindest and most gentle people alive. Everyone who knew her thought she was wonderful. It was almost unimaginable that Eddie could have some grudge against her. But, of course, that was precisely why she was chosen. How better to make Mr. Waters look bad than to make Beth his victim?

Mr. Lane was sure that Eddie had no conception of the damage that his story might do to Beth. Some students would believe the story. Even if they did not, it would not soon be forgotten. Beth would have to live with the humiliation for the next two years. The story was surely very cruel.

Mr. Lane had tried to explain this to Eddie, but Eddie simply could not be gotten to see that words could do people harm. Mr. Lane found Eddie puzzling. He was at the same time talented and tormented, brilliant and immature. Eddie wanted his revenge and was not going to see that it would have a high cost for Beth.

Unfortunately, Eddie was not only a good writer, he was also politically astute. He suspected that Mr. Lane might consider refusing to print his story, so he came to see him prepared with a truckload of arguments about freedom of the press and students' rights. He even managed to work some hints of lawyers and lawsuits into the discussion. Mr. Lane had to admire Eddie's ability to threaten him obliquely.

Mr. Lane did not wish to censor Eddie's story. He was a journalism teacher. He abhorred censorship. He had hoped that Eddie could be persuaded to be responsible about the matter. It would not have been too hard for Eddie to modify his story to make the characters bear no obvious relationship to real people. The role of the faculty adviser was to teach and advise, not censor. Nor did Mr. Lane wish to think about lawyers. If he decided to censor Eddie's story, he supposed that he would have to check out the matter before he did anything, but first he wanted to think it through on its merits.

Should he refuse to allow Eddie's story to be printed? He had never before censored a student publication. Prior to this incident, he thought that he could not imagine a case in which he would. But to refuse to do so would subject Beth to undeserved humiliation. Could he allow that? Mr. Lane decided to sleep on it. Perhaps his duty would be clearer tomorrow.

## DISPUTE

A: In a free society, freedom of speech is a basic and inviolable right. You can't suppress or outlaw what people may say.

B: If that's true, what about laws against libel? Surely we have them to protect people from unjust public defamation of character.

A: That's different. I mean people should be free to say anything that doesn't harm other people.

B: Who is to judge if harm might be done? And what constitutes "harm" anyway? Are revolutionary ideas harmful to the status quo? Does sexually explicit language harm a reader or listener? Is telling someone the unvarnished truth about themselves harmful?

A: I don't know. I only know that the presumption of free speech is essential to openmindedness and to the truth's being heard. It's essential to have all views available so the best may emerge victorious. Suppression of ideas and opinions is the hallmark of a closed society.

B: But we don't stock pornographic books in school libraries, and we don't allow textbooks that are implicitly racist or antifeminist to be used in schools. In our society today, we obviously believe in censorship for the good of others and not in unbridled free expression. We do suppress some opinions and points of view.

A: It seems like that's true, but if the principle of free speech is compromised in that way, what's to stop anyone from coming up with a good protective reason to put down the publication of anything?

B: Nothing, I guess, if you are persuasive enough. Free speech isn't what it's cut out to be once you make exceptions, is it?

A: No. I still feel that it is essential in a free society, but I don't know how to defend it!

## CONCEPTS

Let us look at some of the concepts that are used to justify intellectual freedom and are relevant to this dispute and the case of Mr. Lane and Eddie.

First, we should spend a little time examining the views of John Stuart Mill as expressed in "On Liberty," his classic essay on the subject. Mill summarizes his arguments for what he calls freedom of opinion in the following passage:

> First, if any opinion is compelled to silence, that opinion may, for ought we can certainly know, be true. To deny this is to assume our own infallibility.
>
> Second, though the silenced opinion may be an error, it may, and very often does, contain a portion of the truth; and since the general or prevailing opinion on any subject is rarely or never the whole truth, it is only by the collision of adverse opinions that the remainder of the truth has any chance of being supplied.
>
> Thirdly, even if the received opinion be not only true, but the whole truth, unless it is suffered to be, and actually is rigorously and earnestly contested, it will, by most of those who receive it, be held in the manner of a prejudice, with little comprehension or feeling of its rational grounds. And not only this, but fourthly, the meaning of the doctrine itself will be in danger of being lost or enfeebled, and deprived of its virtual effect on the character and conduct; the dogma becoming a mere formal profession, inefficacious for good, but cumbering the ground and preventing the growth of any real and heartfelt conviction from reason or personal experience.[3]

In this passage Mill constructs an argument for what is sometimes referred to as "the marketplace of ideas." The central contention is that truth is achieved or pursued by means of open criticism and public debate. Institutions such as free speech and freedom of the press are necessary if truth is to be sought and ideas improved. To censor an idea is to deny people the opportunity to consider it, to test their own views against it, and, thus, to learn. Moreover, uncontested ideas atrophy. People who hold to such ideas first lose their sense of the reasons for these ideas and ultimately of what these ideas mean. Uncontested ideas thus degenerate into meaningless cliches.

---

3. John Stuart Mill, *On Liberty* (Indianapolis, IN: Bobbs-Merrill, 1859/1956), p. 64.

It may be worth noting that here Mill is speaking primarily about a social process whereby a society's ideas are examined, refined, and added to. Nevertheless, Mill also argues that freedom is important for personal growth.

Consider the following:

> He who lets the world, or his own portion of it, choose his plan of life for him has no need of any other faculty than the ape-like one of imitation. He who chooses his plan for himself employs all his faculties. He must use observation to see, reasoning and judgment to foresee, activity to gather materials for decision, firmness and self-control to hold to his deliberate decision. And these qualities he requires and exercises exactly in proportion as the part of his conduct which he determines according to judgment and feeling is a large one.[4]

Mill's point seems simple and compelling. Personal growth requires freedom. People who lack the opportunity to make their own decisions also lack the opportunity to develop the capacities to make their own decisions competently. Personal competence requires practice. When we deny to people the right to make their own decisions we deny them the right to grow.

These arguments make a strong case against censoring Eddie's story. To do so would be to interfere with the free marketplace of ideas. It would be to impose one's own judgment concerning what is true or correct upon the process of free exchange of information whereby free people can make such decisions for themselves. Granted that in this case someone will be hurt by publishing the story. But censors always argue that their censorship prevents some greater evil. To accept that argument is to accept the principle that people with power are entitled to impose their view of what is good or true on others whenever they think that it would be best to do so. Do not most censors believe themselves to be doing good? In addition, to censor Eddie's story would be to deny to Eddie the opportunity to be responsible for himself and to grow from his mistakes. The arguments for freedom that Mill provides seem to apply straightforwardly to this case.

Before we give the victory to Eddie too quickly, however, we should first consider another comment by Mill. Having provided his readers with a first formulation of his view of liberty, Mill adds the following qualification:

> It is, perhaps, hardly necessary to say that this doctrine is meant to apply only to human beings in the maturity of their faculties. We are not speaking of children or of young persons below the age which the law may fix as that of manhood or womanhood. Those who are still in a state to require being taken care of by others must be protected against their own actions as well as against external injury.[5]

---

4. Ibid., pp. 71, 72.
5. Ibid., p. 13.

Here Mill claims that the rights he argues for so forcibly for adults do not apply to children and others deemed not legally competent. Why? Generally, the answer is that the consequences of liberty for children are not the same as the consequences of liberty for adults. In the passage quoted, Mill notes that children need to be protected from the consequences of their own actions. Children presumably differ from adults in the degree to which they appreciate the consequences and the significance of their actions. They thus require protection from harmful and unforeseen consequences of their behavior. While Mill does not say so, it is reasonable for us to assume that he would hold that others are likewise deserving of protection from the actions of the immature.

Elsewhere Mill indicates that the benefits normally resulting from liberty do not accrue to the immature, who are not capable of profiting from free and equal discussion. Mill concludes that the immature may have their liberty interfered with provided that the end is their own betterment.

Thus, there is another side to the case. One might argue that Eddie's immaturity disqualifies him from fully participating in the right of a free press. Eddie lacks the maturity to understand the full significance of what his story might do to Beth. Moreover, it is doubtful that in this case the benefits that are supposed to flow from liberty will actually be realized. Springfield students are not likely to be led by Eddie's story to a better understanding of human passion and emotion. More likely, they are going to be led into a lot of ugly gossip and speculation about Mr. Waters and Beth. It is hard to see this as a case of people pursuing truth by means of free and equal discussion.

Nor is it obvious that Eddie will learn from his mistake. Perhaps he will, but it is also easy to believe that when he does he will wish that Mr. Lane had been willing to prevent him from his error. One can also easily imagine that Eddie will be harmed by his story's publication. Certainly many students will be angry about his treatment of Beth. If Eddie cannot handle Mr. Waters's ridicule, how will he deal with rejection by many of his peers? It is possible that the long-range consequences of publishing his story could be quite destructive to Eddie.

It is important to be clear about what really does follow from Mill's argument. Mill is not claiming that children never learn from discussion. Nor is he arguing that children never learn from being permitted to decide things for themselves. His point is not that children need detailed adult control in everything they do. Instead, his point is that adults are permitted to restrict the range of children's freedom for the benefit of the child, whereas such paternalism would be impermissible if directed toward adults. Adults have a right to freedom. They cannot be interfered with for their own good. Children are given freedom by adults when it is believed that it serves the interests of the child. Given this view, the question Mr. Lane must ask is not whether Eddie has a right to publish his story regardless of the consequences, but whether the consequences of allowing Eddie to publish the story are better than the consequences of censoring the story. Which decision will best promote the growth of the students at Springfield High?

## ANALYSIS

Mill's argument is clearly a consequentialist one. It is based on the principle of benefit maximization. Indeed, Mill is quite clear in his essay that he will defend liberty on utilitarian grounds. He will attempt to show that liberty serves the greatest good for the greatest number. To a large extent the force of his defense of free speech and a free press depends on the suggestion that the utility of an idea depends on its truth. Simply put, true ideas contribute more to happiness than false ones.

Likewise, Mill's denial of liberty to those "not in the maturity of their faculties" is given a consequentialist argument. The reason the liberties of adults and children differ is that the consequences of extending liberty to adults and children differ.

The weaknesses of Mill's argument are also the weaknesses of consequentialist arguments in general. In order to know what to do, we must know what the consequences of our actions will be. But who among us really has a clear idea of what the consequences of allowing Eddie to publish his story will be? And how are we to judge the results of censorship?

Mill is willing to allow exceptions to his principles of liberty regarding children because of possibly undesirable consequences. Before we agree or disagree with this, we should consider that the argument may have broader application than to children. For example, in the mid1980s there was extensive media coverage of the adulteration of some common over-the-counter medication with poison. This coverage generated several imitators and eventually cost consumers millions of dollars for the provision of tamper-proof packaging for many items. The consequences of this extensive publicity were quite foreseeable: There have been several similar cases. Moreover, the incident itself was local and hardly as newsworthy as the coverage received would indicate. Before the publicity, the chances of a similar happening elsewhere were slim. The scope of the coverage may have been dictated more by the desire to sell newspapers and television advertising time than by the desire to report significant news. In short, a case can be made that the news media behaved irresponsibly in giving the incident the kind of coverage it received.

One can find numerous other cases in which a free press seems hardly to serve the marketplace of ideas, but does serve commercial interests, often in ways that do genuine harm. Many parents use the television as a babysitter, with the result that preschool children are often raised on a diet of soap operas. The idea that current soap operas provide an important early model of family relationships is, we think, genuinely appalling. One could go on.

Do these abuses and misuses of the right of free speech make a case for censorship? A consequentialist is not committed to saying yes. It is worth noting, however, that the temptation to say yes is there along with the structure of an argument to defend the decision. The principle of benefit maximization tempts one to say that freedom is fine when it has desirable consequences, but not otherwise. Consequentialist ways of thinking can be a threat to liberty. Mill is very optimistic about the desirable effects of liberty, at least for adults. Suppose he is wrong. How much of our own liberty are we willing to forgo because liberty has different consequences than Mill supposed?

Consider a more imaginative, but perhaps more forceful, example. Imagine that in some future time a group of scientists announced that they had discovered a way to make all of humanity infinitely and permanently happy. All that was necessary was for people to turn themselves over to a hospital where they would have electrodes implanted in their brains that would stimulate their pleasure centers on a regular basis. Since they would be blissfully aware only of their own pleasure, they would need to be fed intravenously and would be confined to a hospital bed for the remainder of their days. People need not be concerned about this, however, since the system of maintenance is self-regulating and virtually foolproof.

The government, learning of this plan, did a quick calculation of the average utility and determined that since this plan maximized the happiness of everyone involved the plan would be compulsory. People would not be permitted to deny themselves their ultimate happiness.

The moral is that unqualified emphasis on benefit maximization, given the right facts, can lead not only to the denial of a basic right to freedom of choice, but to the substitution of happiness for growth. Suppose ignorance really is bliss. A consequentialist will prefer bliss.

On this topic Mill expresses the proper sentiment:

> It is better to be a human being dissatisfied than a pig satisfied; better to be Socrates dissatisfied than a fool satisfied. And if the fool, or the pig, are of a different opinion, it is because they only know their side of the question. The other party to the comparison knows both sides.[6]

This is the right thought. The difficulty is that it is hard to justify it with utilitarian arguments. Perhaps, then, there are other reasons to value freedom and human growth over and above happiness.

6. John Stuart Mill, *Utilitarianism*, reprinted in *The Utilitarian* (New York: Doubleday, 1961), p. 410.

Let us look at the issue from a nonconsequentialist point of view. Recall that a central claim of many nonconsequentialist views is that persons are of value because they are moral agents. That people are moral agents who are responsible for themselves and their own conduct has much to say about these issues.

Most importantly, it provides a reason for freedom. If people consider themselves to be moral agents, responsible for their own conduct, then they must insist on the right to act as their choices dictate. To deny a person freedom is to deny that person the opportunity to be a moral agent. It is to fail to show respect for the dignity and worth of that person. People who believe that they are ultimately responsible for what they do cannot allow their choices to be arbitrarily interfered with. Nor will they willingly interfere with the choices of others. They will be willing to restrain others only when others interfere with their own freedom. Generally, however, they will insist on the greatest degree of freedom consistent with an equal amount of freedom for others.

Basic rights such as free speech and a free press can also be defended from this perspective. People who believe that they are responsible for what they do will also demand the conditions of responsible choice. They will insist that they not be denied information that is relevant to their choice, and they will want the opportunity to discuss and debate with others. Free speech and a free press are thus essential components of a society that regards human beings as responsible moral agents.

Personal growth is also an important component of moral responsibility. People who regard themselves as responsible agents will have to value their own competence. Responsible decisions result not only from freely available information, but from the wisdom and capacity to use it. Moral agents, thus, must value their own ability to make reasonable judgments and must as a consequence value their own growth.

Not only will such people value their liberty and growth, but they will not be willing to trade it for their happiness. People who believe that they are responsible for what they do will be unwilling to exchange their freedom for some other benefit, since this might result in their being compelled to do something that violates their moral duty. Part of the philosophical basis of the Nuremberg trials following World War II was the insight that moral agents cannot escape the responsibility of evaluating what they are asked to do. Obeying orders is never an excuse for a moral agent to do evil.

Does this shed any light on what Mr. Lane ought to do about Eddie's story? It might be argued that it does. The above nonconsequentialist arguments seem to make freedom more central to the moral life and prevent us from restricting another person's freedom merely because the consequences of doing so might be better; thus, Mr. Lane should let Eddie's story be published. But what happens if we apply the categorical imperative to the case of immature people?

If we were asked whether we were willing to make interference with other people's choices a universal rule of human conduct, we suppose most of us would refuse. Few of us would be willing to apply such a rule to our own case. We are not willing to be interfered with; thus, universality requires that we not interfere with others. But suppose we ask instead whether there are any conditions under which we might be willing to be interfered with. We might give a somewhat different response.

Most of us would be willing to be interfered with if our judgment was impaired. If we were sleepwalking and were about to fall down the stairs, we would wish to be interfered with. If we were drunk and were about to attempt a spin on the freeway, we would wish to be interfered with. Or if for some reason we were temporarily deranged and were about to commit murder, we would wish to be interfered with.

Moral agents will wish to be interfered with precisely in those cases where they are incapable of acting as moral agents. Competence is a prerequisite of responsible choice. We wish to be interfered with in just those cases about which we will later say that had we been in control, had we known what we were doing, we would have done something else. This is the sort of intervention in another person's choices that is consistent with equal respect for persons. Recall the suggestion that Eddie might eventually come to wish that Mr. Lane had refused to publish the story. This thought ought now to have a new significance. Might not Eddie, in a few years, come to view himself as having been very immature and as having been incapable at the time of fully realizing the significance of his act of vengeance on Mr. Waters?

Maturity remains a relevant consideration, but it has become relevant in a different way. The issue now is whether or not Eddie is in fact mature enough to be held responsible for his actions. Perhaps a good way to test one's insights into this question is to ask whether we are willing to treat Eddie as a responsible adult when it comes to taking the consequences for what he has done. If his story is libelous, are we willing to have him sued as an adult? If we are doubtful, that is reason to wonder if we are really sure that Eddie is adequately capable of a responsible choice.

The nonconsequentialist argument based on the principle of respect for persons is not problem-free. It shares with the consequentialist analysis the difficulty that the notion of maturity is vague. People are not simply mature or immature. Maturity is a many-faceted thing acquired over a long period of time. Any attempt to provide a legal definition will result in drawing a sharp line through territory without clear boundaries. It will be inherently arbitrary. This problem, however, is more severe for the nonconsequentialist. The consequentialist must ask about the consequences of allowing this person to make this choice at this time. These are not always easy questions to answer, but they are asked in a context in which there may be facts relevant to the answer. The nonconsequentialist must ask a more difficult question. It must be decided whether a person is sufficiently competent to be treated as a responsible moral agent. The considerable difficulty our society has with the insanity defense of criminal behavior should suggest the formidable problems involved. It is hard to see how to go about deciding how competent is competent enough.

Finally, an unqualified emphasis on respect for persons has the general difficulty of all nonconsequentialist arguments. It makes consequences irrelevant. Should we decide that Eddie is responsible for his behavior, must it follow that the effects on Beth of publishing his story are irrelevant? Would it not be better to find a way of balancing Eddie's right to be treated as a responsible agent against Beth's right not to be subjected to humiliation? Nonconsequentialist arguments seem to lack a way to account for how effects of behavior are relevant to their moral appraisal. That, however, seems counterintuitive.

## REFLECTIONS ON METHOD

Let us conclude this discussion with these observations.

1.  Note first that this debate is relevant not only to how we view issues of censorship and intellectual liberty, but also to how we see the basic objectives of education. Consequentialists will see education as a means of promoting the good, whatever they take the good to be. If the good is believed to be happiness or success, then consequentialists will see education primarily as a device to promote happiness or success. Thus, consequentialists are likely to have a rather utilitarian conception of the purposes of education. They will value human growth as a means to something else, as a means to promote the greatest good for the greatest number. Nonconsequentialists, however, will see education as a prerequisite to moral agency. It will serve to develop competent and morally responsible persons. Students will be encouraged to decide responsibly who they will be and how they will live with others. Education will be in the business of creating persons.
2.  In this argument about freedom, unlike the previous one about punishment, neither moral theory seems to favor one choice over the other. It seemed clear that if Mr.. Fuse was to defend himself, he would have to rely on consequentialist arguments. In this case, however, Mr. Lane might reach a decision to censor or not by arguing from either theory.

Both moral theories have strong arguments for liberty, and both make maturity a consideration in whether liberty should be extended to children. Finally, both theories suggest reasons why freedom is an important component of an educative environment.

We should not conclude, however, that how we argue or what we decide is a matter of indifference. The basic values—educational values—of these two ways of thinking are different. Moreover, as we hope our imaginary future society will have suggested, these views can make a notable difference in some cases. Sometimes it is no small matter whether we should be willing to trade moral autonomy for happiness. They do not always go hand in hand.

3. Here, as in the previous case, we have not resolved the problem, and we have made frequent appeals to the reader's moral intuitions, again testing the moral theories against what seems to feel right. The results have been inconclusive. But we will have done more than simply test moral theories against intuitive moral judgments. Our deliberations will also have had some effect on what those moral intuitions were. Sometimes the analysis, if it was successful, suggested a new way of seeing the problem or showed that something unsuspected was involved in it. Thus, the moral theories and analyses not only have been tested against moral intuitions, but have actively restructured our moral intuitions and, perhaps, even changed them. This is another piece of evidence to keep in mind concerning the nature of moral reflection. Despite the inconclusive results, the process of analysis has not been powerless over our thinking and moral judgments.

Before going on to the next chapter, you may wish to examine some additional cases. The first one, "Censorship?", lends itself to role playing and developing an empathic understanding of heartfelt challenges to defenses of freedom. The second one, "Alternatives," raises the question of limiting a teacher's free speech.

## ADDITIONAL CASES

### Censorship?

John Corey is the principal of William Heard Kilpatrick Junior High School. He is a conscientious administrator, concerned about the welfare of the students and the quality of the curriculum. He is also an active participant in the meetings of the PTA, and he encourages parental interest in school affairs. He feels that he carries out his duties effectively and serves his institution well.

Mr. Corey's peace was abruptly disturbed one afternoon by an angry phone call from Mrs. Emma Lincoln, the mother of a student. Mrs. Lincoln informed him that she, her husband, their minister, and several other parents had been monitoring the books that their children had brought home from school, and they were very unhappy with some of the selections from the school library.

As an example, she cited one book with which she was familiar, Kurt Vonnegut's *God Bless You, Mr. Rosewater*. This book, according to Mrs. Lincoln, is filled with stories of drunkenness, promiscuity, antisocial behavior, and irreligious thought. This, she said, is poor literature for her children to be reading and an inappropriate part of the school library collection. She added that many other books in the school library fit that same category. She and a committee of concerned parents planned to raise this issue at the next meeting of the PTA. They would demand that the school library collection be reviewed and that these books and other objectionable items be removed. If necessary, they would take legal action. It was their right as parents and taxpayers.

That this issue had arisen among the parents was a complete surprise to Mr. Corey. His first thought was to call Mrs. Jennings, the school librarian. Christine Jennings had been with the school for thirteen years, had compiled most of the book collection, and was a valued member of the staff. She had a reputation for being conservative in social matters and was acquainted with many of the parents. She would know how to placate them.

Mr. Corey was shocked by her angry response and flat rejection of the case presented by Mrs. Lincoln. In Mrs. Jennings's view, *God Bless You, Mr. Rosewater* was a minor classic of recent American literature that should be included in any school library. It celebrated human frailty, the humble civic virtues, and the possibility of kindness in an unkind world. According to Mrs. Jennings, it was this sort of work to which the students ought to be exposed, and she would make this argument in favor of any book the parents might select from her library. That her handling of the library would be questioned at all was a personal insult she would not accept. Furthermore, in her opinion, no group had the right to censor a library, and she was prepared to fight in defense of that position. With that, she hung up the telephone.

Mr. Corey gently replaced the receiver in its cradle. Much had happened in a brief part of the afternoon. An issue had arisen that could seriously disrupt the peace of the school and extend beyond its walls. A group of parents was up in arms, and his librarian had wrapped herself in the Bill of Rights. It was his responsibility to salve the anger of the parties in this dispute, yet still carry out his duties as principal. Mr. Corey had no strong opinion about the books in question, but he had to arrange a compromise. The next PTA meeting was a week away.

The meeting only exacerbated the problem. The parents had planned their strategy and presented a united front. The Reverend Campbell, the Lincolns' pastor, served as their spokesman. He presented a list of titles that the group found to be offensive, including Vonnegut's *God Bless You, Mr. Rosewater* and *Slaughterhouse Five*, Joseph Heller's *Catch22*, and J. D. Salinger's *The Catcher in the Rye.* The Reverend Campbell claimed that these books were obscene, un-American, and, in an insidious way, introduced a secular humanism into the school. The parents had the right to protect their children in such matters and make their opinions felt. It was their demand that such books as the parents' committee might select be removed from the library and that they have the right to review the place of such works in the school curriculum.

Mrs. Jennings spoke for herself and a number of the teachers. It was their position that parental intervention in the library or the school curriculum would be censorship, a violation of academic freedom. Such a situation would indeed be un-American. They would stand for no interference.

No dialogue developed, and the meeting became a shouting match. Mr. Corey called an adjournment and promised that he and the school board would attempt to reach a compromise on the issue.

After much discussion, Mr. Corey and the school board submitted a possible compromise to a later meeting of parents and teachers. The provisions of the plan were:

1.  No books would be removed from the library, and no changes would be required in the curriculum at that time.
2.  A parent could request, in writing, that a student be prevented from taking certain books from the library.
3.  If the parents found a certain work to be offensive, the student could be excused from the assignment and allowed to leave the classroom.
4.  A committee of concerned parents and teachers would be created in order to review new acquisitions for the library and recommend any changes in the curriculum.

Both parties rejected the compromise. The Reverend Campbell stated that the proposal did not resolve the original problem and avoided very real moral issues. He could not sanction the presence of books in the library that were morally objectionable. It was his duty to protect all the students, not just a few. Furthermore, the parents who chose to participate in the new program would subject their children to the implied criticism of their teachers and the ridicule of their classmates. This would be harmful and uneducative for the students. The Reverend Campbell announced that the parents intended to file suit against the school board and were willing to keep their children out of school unless the principal removed the objectionable books from the library. They would elect a more compliant school board, if necessary.

Mrs. Jennings charged that the new plan only served to establish a form of censorship. It was the teachers' position that the Reverend Campbell and his group had no right to impose a single point of view on a public institution. The school board's proposal was an insult to the librarian's taste and the teachers' professionalism. They would not abandon their legitimate control over the classroom and yield to outside pressure. The teachers were prepared to file a countersuit against the parents and might even strike to protect their academic freedom.

What can Mr. Corey do in order to help resolve this problem?

*Some Questions*

1.  Try role playing this case. Imagine a public meeting where all the major characters plus some students and teachers are allowed to present their points of view. After all have spoken, analyze each argument to see what principles are being used to justify a position. Which arguments seem to have the most merit? Why?
2.  Write a plausible ending to this case. Compare your ending with that of others. Do all of these endings occur in real life? What factors might make the most desirable ending most probable?
3.  The problem of the maturity of students is a constant one for teachers. Can you formulate any standards, principles, or rules that might help teachers make finer judgments about what is and is not appropriate material for students of different school or grade levels?

## Alternatives

The idea of an alternative school is not a new one, but this was the first time Marple Grove was trying to use it to solve the persistent problem of senior slump. Once students found they were accepted into a college, especially after early decisions, finishing the year of regular high school work was not particularly appealing.

Everyone went through the motions, with some exceptions. A few were so lax they found themselves failing a required subject, and there were some close calls at graduation. Most, however, just coasted, including the teachers. It was just an accepted part of the school culture at Marple Grove.

Last year, however, a small group of teachers found themselves wondering about the waste of time and talent, their own included, that resulted from senior slump. Wouldn't it be more educationally beneficial if they could provide an alternative to work as usual in their regular classes for those who had applied to college, an alternative school within a school that was educationally sound and yet different enough to be interesting and challenging?

They put their heads together and came up with an exciting proposal that they presented to Mrs. Zinna, the principal. It was unusual, but with careful structuring and monitoring, it would meet state requirements. Mrs. Zinna felt strongly that it was worth a try. She invited the two teachers who had emerged as leaders of the group to present the plan to the school board.

They convinced the board that a carefully controlled, educationally safe, and thoroughly accountable experiment with the alternative school plan was worth a try. An experimental program was approved, with the proviso of careful reviewing and revoting at the end of two years.

Ms. Winsome and Mr. Losesome were the two lead teachers. A year had passed, and things seemed to be going well for the twenty students selected for the experiment. The parents were pleased with the serious involvement of their sons and daughters in the program. The teachers felt they had really found the solution to the problem. The students enjoyed being treated differently and having an unusual curriculum for their last half-year.

Ms. Winsome felt it was a waste of time to wait another year before making the alternative an opportunity for all seniors, not just a few. She went to Mrs. Zinna to try to persuade her, but the principal took her promise to the board and her integrity as an administrator-researcher as reasons to stay with the original plan. Hard evidence of success, based on successful replication the second year, was a better basis for approving the program for all students than the intuitions and subjective judgments of a lead teacher. Mr. Losesome agreed with Mrs. Zinna.

Ms. Winsome was fit to be tied. She knew in her bones that she was right. It was not fair to deny the entire next senior class what clearly was a better kind of education. However, she knew it would be wrong to go over Mrs. Zinna's head to the board herself. It seemed like such a waste, though.

Then an idea hit her that seemed to provide the solution. After all, free speech and freedom of the press were principles she and other social studies teachers extolled all the time. She would write a letter to the local paper as an individual citizen reporting on her very positive feelings about the alternative school and urge other concerned citizens to petition the board to make it a regular and full part of the high school program next year.

This was a perfect solution! She even fantasized that groups would come to the board meeting to present their own ideas; and in that "free marketplace of ideas," the truth would win out more quickly than in some closed and narrow experimental process. She saw herself as a free citizen acting responsibly in her community and serving the public good. She lifted her pen and began, "To the Editor..."

*Some Questions*

1.  Can you think of situations or circumstances in which the free speech of teachers in their role as professionals should be curtailed? When do individual rights give way to professional obligations? Do you think Ms. Winsome did the right thing?
2.  Look at the NEA Code. Is there any provision in it relevant to this case? Do professionals have special obligations to other professionals?
3.  Is there a clash between the process of a free marketplace producing truth and experiment producing truth? In this case, are we most concerned with moral truth, scientific truth, or educational truth? Are these different things with different processes for arriving at them?

## FOR FURTHER INQUIRY

American Civil Liberties Union. http://www.aclu.org/studentsrights/expression/index.html
    The ACLU is a civil rights organization. This link takes you to a page concerning student rights and free expression.

Berlin, Isaiah. *Four Essays on Liberty.* London: Oxford University Press, 1969.
    Four classical essays on the nature and importance of liberty.

Fischer, Louis, David Schimmel, and Leslie R. Stellman. *Teachers and the Law.* 6th ed. Boston: Allyn and Bacon, 2003, Chapter 9.
    A good resource for the law on the right of free expression for teachers and students.

*Hazelwood School District et al.* v. *Kuhlmeier et al.,* 484 U.S. 260 (1988), (1988).
    A Supreme Court case that reduced the scope of *Tinker* v. *Des Moines.*

Mill, John Stuart. *On Liberty.* New York: The Bobbs-Merrill Company, inc., 1859/1956.
    The classical statement of the arguments for freedom and individuality. Chapter 2 emphasizes liberty of thought and discussion.

Strike, K. A. *Liberty and Learning.* Oxford, England: M. Robertson, 1981.
    A discussion of the importance of freedom in education.

Strike, K. (1985). A field guide of censors: Toward a concept of censorship in schools. *Teachers College Record, 87*:2, 239–258.
    A discussion of censorship in education

*Tinker* v. *Des Moines Independent School District* 393 U.S. 503.
    The lead Supreme Court precedent on student rights.

# Chapter 4

# Equal Opportunity and Democratic Community

The NEA Code also holds that the educator:

6.  Shall not on the basis of race, color, creed, sex, national origin, marital status, political or religious beliefs, family, social or cultural background, or sexual orientation, unfairly:
    a.  Exclude any student from participation in any program;
    b.  Deny benefits to any student;
    c.  Grant any advantage to any student.

## A TALE OF TWO MEETINGS:
## TWO CASES TO CONSIDER

### Case 1: Honors Algebra

Elizabeth Teal sat in a meeting with Teshan Williams, his parents, and the principal of Roosevelt High, Candice Weaver. The agenda was whether Teshan would be allowed to enroll in her honors algebra class. Technically Teshan was not eligible. Ms. Weaver was opposed. "If we make an exception for him, we'll have to do it for everyone," she argued; moreover, "if we start admitting weak students this will have an effect on what you can do with the other students in the class. Pretty soon it won't be an honors class. We have to protect this class." But Teshan wanted in, and his parents were adamant.

Algebra is a gate keeper course everywhere. Students who don't take it or don't pass it are unlikely to go to college. At Roosevelt, Teshan would have to take algebra. It was mandated for all ninth graders in his state. But at Roosevelt honors algebra was a gate keeper in a different way. The kids who took the regular algebra class at Roosevelt typically were poorly prepared to succeed and often were not particularly motivated. Many failed. They were disproportionately among the 35% of Roosevelt students who dropped out. Those who passed usually would take no more math. If they went to college it would be the local community college where they often dropped out before completing a program. The standards in these classes were pretty low. The kids who took honors algebra, however, were the ones who took more math in high school and who went to four-year institutions—sometimes even elite schools. Honors algebra was a powerful sorter at Roosevelt. Its role seemed to be to select those students who had potential and to separate them from the rest so as to give them an education that would allow them to go to college. Teshan's parents knew this. That's why they had asked for the meeting. They wanted their son to be able to go to a good college. They saw this as a high stakes decision for Teshan.

The problem was that Teshan wasn't well prepared to succeed in honors algebra. His junior high grades in math were undistinguished. Teshan had come to Roosevelt from Kennedy Junior High. Few students from Kennedy came adequately prepared to do honors algebra. Because it did not completely trust the grades from its two feeder schools, Roosevelt also gave a screening math test to its entering students and used it to determine placement. Teshan had done better than most other students from Kennedy, but he was still below the cut line for admission into her class. Moreover, the class was full and there were other students who hadn't made the cut, but who had better grades and higher scores than Teshan. Most of these students came from Truman, the other feeder school for Roosevelt.

Teshan's parents made the case for him. It went like this: "Teshan is a talented boy. In junior high he didn't work very hard, and the student culture in Kennedy was not supportive. Moreover, he wasn't very well taught. You know that Kennedy has problems. Still he did better than most. While he didn't score above the cut line, he is close, and if he had been competently taught he probably would have done better than many students from Truman. We have talked with him, and he understands doing well in your class is important. We will be sure that he works hard in your class. It is not his fault that he attended a poor middle school. He deserves this chance."

Ms. Teal agreed that it was likely that had Teshan attended Truman, he probably would have done better. Students from Truman always seemed well taught. They were the overwhelming majority in her honors class. And probably with his parents support and extra work on her part Teshan would pass. He might even do well. She probably could take another student. And Teshan was African American. Ms. Teal wondered if this was also a reason why he deserved a chance. She felt some sympathy for her African American students, especially those from Kennedy, who often seemed to come to Roosevelt poorly prepared. They frequently didn't have the same chance to succeed as did white students. But was this a reason to give Teshan a chance she might not have given a white student from Truman?

## Susan's Third Grade

Ms. Cleaver sat in a meeting with several of the parents of her third grade students. Oddly they weren't exactly there to complain that she treated their children badly. In fact, they seemed to be pretty happy about most things. They were there to complain that she treated Susan too well. Susan was blind. She was a sweet child whom everyone liked. But she was also painfully shy, and because she was blind she was easily omitted from classroom activities.

Ms. Cleaver had made it a project to ensure that Susan was included. She avoided activities in which Susan had difficulty participating. For example, in physical education, she tended to emphasize relay races over the ever popular dodge ball. She would have one student hold Susan's hand while she ran. She didn't see how she could include Susan in dodge ball. In class she minimized the visual arts and emphasized music.

Ms. Cleaver provided a lot of encouragement for the students in her class to include Susan in whatever they did. She often asked for volunteers to help Susan in some group activity. She would always make sure that Susan got an opportunity to talk. Sometimes Ms. Cleaver provided Susan with a great deal of individualized instruction. She didn't keep track with a stop watch, but she estimated that about 25% of her class time was spent helping Susan. She had even begun to learn to read Braille so she could help Susan. Susan had a special teacher who helped her to read Braille, but that teacher wasn't in her class enough.

Most of the parents who had asked for the meeting were happy to have Susan in the class with their children. But at some point they had been concerned with the amount of time Ms. Cleaver spent with her. This was time that she didn't spend with their children. One of the parents also worried about the special status Susan had and the encouragement Ms. Cleaver gave their children to help her. "It's fine," one parent said, "to make sure Susan is included, but you've made my child into an unpaid assistant." Others were concerned that limiting various classroom activities to those that Susan could participate in was overly restrictive. Mr. Arnold summed up the matter. "We are in favor of equality for disabled students, and we think Susan should be in your class, but you have made her so central in what goes on that we feel that our children are deprived of your time and of the wide range of lessons and activities they should enjoy. When was the last time you asked our kids to draw a picture?" Ms. Cleaver did see their point.

## DISPUTE

A: One of the things I appreciate most about our schools in our democratic society is their commitment to providing equal educational opportunity for each and every student.

B: What I have appreciated about our schools in our democratic society is their commitment to including all kinds of students regardless of their differences.

A: I'm not sure what it means to include everyone unless it means that all are treated equally. That's what justice and fairness demand. Ethical educators must make equity one of their central decision-making principles.

B: But do we in education really treat people equally? We give some students A's and others D's. And we admit those students who get A's to elite colleges and deny admission to those who get D's. We provide compensatory education to poor children. We give special educational opportunities to the gifted because we think they deserve them and to the disabled because we think they need them. This isn't treating people equally. It's treating them quite differently.

A: Treating people differently is a problem only if you think equal treatment means providing people the same treatment regardless of relevant differences. After all we give some students A's because they have reached a higher level of achievement than D students. Equity and fairness demand paying attention to those differences that make a difference. We treat everyone equally when we recognize that high talent children and high needs children should have different educational programs because they are *relevantly* different.

B: So equal treatment isn't important. Differences are?

A: No, I didn't say that. Equal treatment means treating people the same unless some relevant difference exists. But it also means that we must recognize relevant differences with different treatment. If two students do the same quality work they should get the same grade. If they do different quality work they should get different grades. And it is especially important that you not treat people differently because of some characteristic such as race that shouldn't ever be used as a reason for different treatment. Equality means not giving higher grades or more opportunity to people because they are members of a favored or disfavored group.

B: So equality means treating people the same if they are the same in some relevant way, and it means treating them differently if they are different in some relevant way?

A: Precisely!

B: And some characteristics such as race, gender, or family income shouldn't ever count as reasons for treating people differently.

A: Now you've got it!

B: Not really. I feel like I'm playing "Who's on first?" Let me try this different way. Let's take the compensatory education. Don't we sometimes use race or family income as reasons for giving compensatory education to some and not others? And consider gifted or disabled students. You claim that they are relevantly different. But gifted students get more resources because they are more talented, and disabled students get more resources because they need them more. Isn't this inconsistent? And is it fair to take limited educational resources away from children who are not gifted or disabled and give them to these "special" groups? Why should those who are "average" have to give up some of the educational benefits they might have gotten so that those who are more naturally endowed or who are more needy can have more? That seems like inequity of the highest order!

A: Well so far as compensatory education is concerned, I think that justice demands that we give those who have been deprived a chance to catch up with others so they can become the real equals of others.

B: Well maybe. Perhaps just societies should occasionally take from the rich and give to the poor. But supporting gifted education seems more like taking from the poor and giving to the rich! How can you justify that?

A: Benefit maximization! The gifted are society's greatest human resource. They are our future doctors and medical researchers, our scientists and engineers, our educators and political leaders. In the long run, given the best education, they will improve the lives of all of us the most.

B: I'm still confused. If this is true shouldn't we give less to disabled students if they are less likely to make effective use of it? How do you know when a difference is a relevant difference? And how do you know how people who are relevantly different should be treated?

A: Well – Ah – I think maybe this is harder than I thought.

B: Maybe! And when we are sorting people into all of these different groups with different treatments and different resources so that we can treat them equally aren't we fragmenting our democratic community? Maybe we should worry less about fair treatment and more about democratic inclusion!

A: But we don't include everyone by treating everyone the same. That would be like teaching everyone in English even though some students spoke only Spanish. So inclusion means recognizing differences.

B: So we treat people differently in order to treat them equally, and we sort them into groups in order to include them. I have a headache.

## CONCEPTS

In the landmark ruling, *Brown* v. *Board of Education*,[7] Chief Justice Warren wrote these words:

> Segregation of white and colored children in public schools has a detrimental effect upon the colored children. The impact is greater when it has the sanction of the law, for the policy of separating the races is usually interpreted as denoting the inferiority of the negro group. A sense of inferiority affects the motivation of a child to learn. Segregation with the sanction of law, therefore, has a tendency to [retard] the educational and mental development of negro children and to deprive them of some of the benefits they would receive in a racial[ly] integrated school system.

*Brown* v. *Board* has had an enormous impact on American education. Not only did it launch the desegregation of American schools, it began a deep and pervasive examination of inequality in many areas of American life. Its influence quickly was extended to issues of gender equality, sexual orientation and of fairness for linguistic minorities and disabled people. *Brown* helped to create the context in which we can think about both of our two cases.

*Brown* is not without its complexities. Our cases suggest two of them. Ms. Teal's reasons for wanting to admit Teshan to her class seems to grant Teshan a benefit on account of his race. The NEA Code seems to forbid this. Does *Brown*? And *Brown* seems to require that we treat people the same regardless of race, however, in the case of Susan, we have a student who is importantly different. She would not benefit from being treated the same as sighted students. What do we owe her?

*Brown* also raises issues of interpretation. It might be read in two ways. One reading sees it as a demand for equality of educational opportunity for African American children. *Brown's* argument for equality appeals to a psychological theory that sees segregation as leading to a sense of inferiority on the part of African American children and connects this sense of inferiority with educational outcomes and life prospects. It says that segregation is illegal because it does educational harm.

Consider a worry about this view of *Brown*. This psychological theory may not be true. Do we want the case for equal rights for African Americas to depend on controversial psychological theories? Suppose they were false. Would we be willing to conclude that segregation of some American citizens is morally acceptable if it did not do educational harm? We doubt this.

---

7. *Brown* v. *Board of Education*, 347 U.S. 483 (1954)

Another way to read *Brown* is that it expresses a more fundamental view of what is central to a democratic community. A genuinely democratic community is one that values all of its members and values them all equally. It grants to each individual a full measure of dignity and respect. The problem with segregation is that it is rooted in the devaluation of one class of citizens by another. And it presumes that it is acceptable to translate this devaluation into institutions in which black Americans are involuntarily separated from white Americans. *Brown* rejects these assumptions of the lack of worth and of the political inferiority of African Americans and asserts their right to be valued and valued equally with white Americans. It is not just about equal educational opportunity and the educational consequences of segregation. It is about equal worth, equal dignity, and equal citizenship.

We think that these comments about *Brown* suggest two lenses through which we can consider our cases. One emphasizes equal opportunity. The second broadens this concern to a concern for democratic community. We will return to these two lenses shortly.

What our two cases have in common is that both concern the relevance of difference. The two students in these cases both have characteristics that distinguish them apart from other students. One student, Teshan, is an African American in a school where the majority is white. The second student, Susan, has a disability. Thus we have to ask whether these differences provide any justification for different treatment for Teshan and for Susan and, if they do, what kinds of different treatment is warranted?

A second thing they have in common is that they concern the distribution of scarce resources. In the first case, we want to know whether the fact that Teshan is a member of a minority group is a reason why he should be admitted to an honors class in algebra. The honors class is a scarce resource. Not everyone who wants to be in this class can be in it, and there are other students some of whom have better qualifications than Teshan, who want to be admitted. Also, if he is admitted, Teshan's presence in the class may mean that Ms. Teal will have to spend more time with him than other students because he is less well prepared, and it may mean that the class will progress more slowly. Thus, if Teshan is admitted, not only may that be unfair to other students with better qualifications who are not, but Ms Teal may be benefiting him at the expense of other students. The honors class and the quality of the honors class both concern competition for scarce resources.

In the second case, one scarce resource is teacher time. Ms. Cleaver spends a lot of time with Susan. This is time that she does not spend with other students. Is this difference in time spent justified by Susan's disability? Moreover, Ms. Cleaver has changed her class in a way that benefits Susan, but that some parents believe deprives their children of a suitably enriched education. The nature of instruction is a resource, and different kinds of instruction may benefit different children differently. If so, it may be that Ms. Cleaver has changed her class in a way that benefits Susan at the expense of other children.

These are all issues of what philosophers call *distributive justice.* The various institutions of society distribute things that people want, but which are scarce. They distribute jobs, income, status, and power. They may do so justly or unjustly. Schools are one institution among others that distribute such goods. As teachers or future teachers, it is important that you notice that your time and your instructional style are also scarce resources that can be distributed fairly or unfairly. How are such problems thought about?

Let us start with a definition of justice proposed by Aristotle (384–322 B.C.). Aristotle held that justice consists in treating equals equally and unequals unequally. What Aristotle meant by treating equals equally is that people who are the same vis-à-vis some relevant characteristic are entitled to be treated in the same way. For example, if previous math grades and the score on a math screening test are relevant grounds for admission into an honors algebra class, then two students with the same grades and scores should receive the same treatment. Either both should be admitted or both should be rejected to honors algebra.

However, when people differ on some relevant characteristic they should be treated differently. A visually disabled student such as Susan is not being treated fairly by being given the same printed book to read as a sighted student. Here fairness requires that we respond to relevant differences with different treatment. Each student should receive reading material from which that student can profit. That requires different kinds of reading material for the visually disabled.

These ideas generate two kinds of questions that we must be able to answer if they are to be sensibly applied. First, we need to know what is to count as a relevant characteristic. Intuitively, so far as education is concerned, it seems as though such things as a student's needs, interests, and ability to profit from instruction are relevant differences. However, characteristics such as race and sex (and all the other characteristics in the part of the NEA Code of Ethics quoted at the beginning of this chapter) would seem to be irrelevant.

If race is an irrelevant characteristic, then it would seem as though the conclusion we should draw about Teshan is that we should not admit him into the honors algebra class. If we treat him as we treat others with similar qualifications, we will not. The fact that he is a member of a particular racial group should make no difference. But stay tuned. There is more to say about this.

In Susan's case, we do have an important relevant difference. Susan is blind. Justice would seem to require different treatment. But what kind of different treatment, and for what reasons? The suggestion that she needs to learn to read Braille seems an obvious one. That is the only way in which she can read at all. The printed word is of no use to her.

But does her disability entitle her to more of her teacher's time than other students receive? Moreover, Susan also benefits from a special teacher who comes in regularly to help her. This teacher costs her school money. This is money not spent on resources for other children. Time and money are scarce resources. What one gets another does not. It may be that Susan needs more of Ms. Cleaver's time, but when does providing more time become unfair to the children who get less time?

We can begin to discuss these issues, by discussing the two lenses that we said were different ways to read *Brown*: equality of educational opportunity and democratic community.

When we aim at creating equal educational opportunity, we think of education as providing fair competition for goods in our society that are allocated by markets and that depend on education. Societies with market-based economies accept the legitimacy of differences in status and income that depend on relative success in economic competition. At the same time we want that competition to be fair. We want equal opportunity. This is what is emphasized in the passage from *Brown* quoted above. Segregation harms achievement, and, in our society, achievement is important to success. *Brown* does not ask for equal income or even equal achievement. It asks for a level playing field.

Equal opportunity has two parts. First, we want a society where success in economic life depends on realized talent rather than on what one looks like or who ones parents are. If so, we must hire people on the basis of the fact that they possess the relevant qualifications for a position. It is okay to hire one person for an engineering job because that person is a better engineer than other applicants. It is not fair to hire that person because of race, parental wealth, or gender. But this is not enough. If the competition for those goods that are allocated by markets is to be fair, we must also give everyone a fair opportunity to acquire those skills that the job market rewards. This is a basic role of public schools.

There is a second lens. We also want to create a democratic community. When we talk about a democratic community, we are not just talking about creating a form of government in which leaders are elected. We are also speaking of creating a community in which everyone is equally valued and is treated with equal respect and dignity. One test of such a community is how it cares for its weakest and most vulnerable members. When we think about education in this way, we don't just ask what we must do to create fair competition. We ask what we must do so that everyone is treated as an equal member of the community regardless of the talents and abilities they possess and regardless of the disabilities that hinder their progress.

One significant difference between these two lenses is how we encourage students to see one another. Equal opportunity is about fair competition. Here students are competitors with one another for such things as grades, further educational opportunity and ultimately jobs and income. Teachers need not place emphasis on this fact or encourage students to view one another in this way. But it is a fact about our society and our schools. However, when we seek to create a democratic community, we do not view one another as competitors. Rather we take the stance that we are all in this together. We emphasize the common good, and we try to ensure that we care for the weakest among us.

Suppose we now consider our cases both as issues about equal opportunity and about democratic community. Does the ideal of equality of opportunity suggest that Teshan should be admitted to the honors algebra class, or not. It might initially seem that it suggests that he should not be admitted. As the NEA Code says, equality of opportunity means that we should not grant any advantage to any student on account of race. Ms. Teal has considered admitting Teshan to her class even though he has not met the qualifications because he is African American. We should certainly not deny a benefit to Teshan because he is African American, but neither should we grant one.

This conclusion may be premature. It may also be argued that Teshan has not met the qualifications for admission into honors algebra because he was not provided with equal educational opportunity earlier in his school career. We suggested that the education he received at Kennedy was inferior to the education other students received at Truman. Moreover, Kennedy has more poor and minority students than does Truman. Perhaps, then we might conclude that Teshan was not provided with equal opportunity in middle school and that this fact is at least associated with his race.

If we conclude this, what follows? Generally what we expect when an injustice has been committed is that a remedy will be provided that restores the victim to the position that he or she would have enjoyed had not the injustice occurred. We might argue that had Teshan received the quality of instruction students receive at Truman, he would have been qualified for Ms. Teal's class. If so, then in order to remedy this inequality, we should restore him to the position he would have had if the injustice had not occurred. We should admit him to Ms. Teal's class. This is a matter of compensatory justice. Perhaps reasoning of this sort is behind Ms. Teal's sympathy for African American students from Kennedy.

How might we look at Teshan's case from the perspective of democratic community? Consider the following argument: One characteristic of a genuinely democratic community is that all of its members are equally valued. Suppose, however, that when we look at a particular community, what we see is that some individuals in that community systematically occupy less favored or disfavored positions. What message is communicated by this? The message that seems communicated is that some people are more highly valued than others.

Notice what we are saying here. We are suggesting that institutions and practice have expressive or communicative aspects to them. They "speak" to the beliefs and attitudes on which they are based. And we can evaluate them by what the express.

Often in the United States our institutions seem to say that we do not value minorities or poor people equally with others. African Americans, for example, are far more likely to be poor, more likely to be unemployed, more likely to live in substandard housing, and more likely to be in jail than are white people. When we look at prestigious positions we find that African Americans are systematically underrepresented. There are fewer African American doctors, lawyers, engineers, or CEOs. When we look at schools what we find is that schools are highly segregated by race. Predominately African American schools tend to be less well funded than predominately white schools, and where schools are more integrated African Americans are disproportionally in the lower tracks. In almost all American schools honors and AP courses are whiter than the school at large. Here the question we want to ask is "What does this say about the extent to which we are a democratic community that values everyone and values all equally?" What it seems to say is that white people are more valued by society that black people.

Note the parallel here to our two readings of *Brown*. If we think of *Brown* as largely about equality of opportunity, we must be interested in the consequences of schooling for achievement and life prospects. But if we think of *Brown* as about democratic community, we are also interested in what is expressed about who is valued and who is not.

If we view Teshan's case as about democratic community, we can make another kind of argument for admitting Teshan to honors algebra. We can say that admitting Teshan to the honors algebra class rectifies what we might call an expressive injustice and helps to constitute us as a more fully democratic society. An honors class which is disproportionately white says something about us. It says that American society values white people more than we value black people. When we take steps to make the racial composition of each of our institutions one that looks more like the society at large, we say convey a different message. We say that all are valued and are valued equally. Admitting Teshan, thus, may be justified because it is a step in the direction of a more democratic society.

There is much more that could be said about these ideas. They do not apply just to African Americans. They apply to all disfavored groups. It is also important that although Teshan has not met the cut score for entry into Ms. Teal's class, he is able to do the work. We do not remedy injustices by putting people in a position where they are bound to fail. We should notice that there may be other Kennedy students who have been disadvantaged by poor instruction for whom the same arguments could be made, but their case is not being considered because their parents have not made it. If we owe Teshan something, we owe them something as well. Finally, there is the question of whether there are group rights. We do not address this issue, but our argument does not depend on any such idea. We do not hold that Teshan has any special claim on resources simply because he is African American. Rather we observe that many African Americans are subject to structural disadvantages and that thus the use of race as a criterion to identify those who have been treated unjustly is prima facie reasonable. At the end of the day, we do think there is a case that can be made for admitting Teshan to Ms. Teal's honors algebra class. We leave it to you to decide if it is a convincing case.

Susan's case is complex for other reasons. That equal opportunity requires that Susan be taught to read Braille seems clear. Equality does not require that we treat everyone exactly the same. It means that we treat them appropriately. We think that at a minimum this means that Susan is entitled to receive instruction in a form from which she can profit. We also think that if her profiting from this different instruction requires more resources than are available to other students, then she is entitled to more resources. We do not know how to decide how much more is too much more. We do not believe that we are obligated to provide Susan with whatever resources are required to enable her to read as well as she might have been able to read were she not blind, and we should not be willing to secure marginal achievement gains for Susan at the expense of significant losses for other students. (We also doubt that exchanges of this sort frequently occur.) So we think Susan is entitled to more resources to enable her to succeed. We do not know how much more is too much.

We think the case for the steps Ms. Cleaver has taken to fully include Susan in the class can best be justified by appealing to the notion of creating a democratic community. Consider two features of such a community. The first is that we must value all and value them equally. This includes those who are the weakest among us. In a democratic community we value people because they are people, not because they are attractive or have high potential. If one test of a genuinely democratic classroom is that it views all students as equal members regardless of race, another is our willingness and ability to fully include students with disabilities. Ms. Cleaver has worked hard to make her classroom a place where Susan is fully included. We think the value of democratic community justifies these steps.

A second feature of democratic community is that its members share those values that are foundational to such communities. Key among these values is that we respect the dignity of everyone. Ms. Cleaver's attempts to include Susan not only are attempts to respect her dignity; they are attempts to teach others to do so as well. She is creating a democratic classroom by a form of moral education that teaches the core values of democratic community to her students. Other students benefit from this.

## ANALYSIS

In our discussion of these cases, we viewed them as cases of distributive justice. They concern the justice of social institutions that determine who gets what in our society. Issues of distributive justice come into play when decisions involve trades between what one person gets and what another gets. Both of our cases involve such trades. If Teshan is admitted to the honors algebra class someone else may not be, and his admission will have consequences for others in the class. The time that Susan is provided is time that others will not get, and the character of the class benefits her but may be less appropriate for others. When we encounter such cases, it is always useful to ask whether we can transform them so that they become "win–win" situations, but that is often not possible. Then we must choose between the welfare of some and the welfare of others.

Consequentialist views provide some distinct ways to analyze these issues.

Reasoning from the principle of benefit maximization will start from the conviction that decisions about how resources are to be allocated must be made in terms of what promotes the greatest good for the greatest number. What distribution of educational resources will enhance the average welfare? Of course it is difficult to answer this question apart from some idea of what kinds of benefits we are interested in maximizing and who our choices effect. The choices we make about Teshan and Susan may have consequences for their families and other loved one, for other students in the class and the school, and for many people who may interact with them over many years. Consequences are like ripples in a pond they expand forever. Many of these consequences are unknowable.

The choices we are considering may also have consequences for quite different kinds of benefits. They may influence achievement, college admission, friendship patterns, and the development of character. It is hard to compare these different consequences or to reduce them to happiness.

Thus, if we want to use the principle of benefit maximization, we will need to make some simplifying assumptions. We can simplify our cases here by stipulating the benefits we are interested in and the people whose welfare we will consider. Suppose, then, that we assume that we are interested in the consequences of our choices for the class in which Susan is being taught and, in the case of Teshan, for the other students who are to take algebra. We will consider two kinds of benefits. We will emphasize the effects on average achievement. However, because we are often interested in achievement because we think that it has economic consequences, we will also make some assumptions about the effects of our decision on our nation's prosperity.

Looked at with these kinds of simplifications, the principle of benefit maximization can give an account of whether we should take race into account in making educational decisions. Generally, race should not be considered because race has nothing to do with whether a person can make effective use of an educational opportunity. To make opportunities available on the basis of race is, therefore, to distribute them in an inefficient way. As a result of an inefficient use of resources, children (on average) will learn less. From the perspective of benefit maximization the primary justification for equality of opportunity, is that inequality is inefficient. And, in fact it usually is.

How do we use resources to maximize achievement? The suggestion implicit in what was just said is that we should focus on the ability to profit from instruction. When we allocate educational resources on the basis of ability to profit, we are putting them where they will do everyone the most good. We admit some people to medical school and not others, for example, because we believe that those we admit are better able to profit from training and will make better doctors than those whom we do not admit. We all benefit from improving the quality of the medical profession. We do not admit people to medical school on the basis of race because race is unrelated to a person's ability to profit from medical instruction and to become a good physician.

Reasoning of this sort is very likely the justification for having an honors algebra class at all. We have an honors class because we think that concentrating a special resource on those students most able to benefit from it makes us all better off. When we do this we hope that the consequence will be that these students will be able to undertake further education that will enable them to develop their skills further and to take on important positions where their work will benefit everyone. This is what we seem to assume when we argue that such honors classes are important if we are to have enough scientists and engineers and if we are to succeed in international economic competition.

Is this a good argument? Consider some challenges to it. First, in the argument above, we suggested that we emphasize allocating resources to those most able to profit from them, because *everyone* benefits. But this is not necessarily true, and it is not what the principle of benefit maximization requires. It may be that giving more resources to those with more ability to profit will increase average achievement, but it may also lessen the achievement of less able students who will get fewer resources as a consequence. And, while these students may be less able to profit from educational resources, they also may need them more. So while we may be able to increase *average* achievement by providing more able students with more resources, raising the average may also harm some students. This is perfectly consistent with the principle of benefit maximization which does not require that we make everyone better off. It requires that we make people better off on the average.

Second, one of the simplifications we accepted in trying to apply the principle of benefit maximization to education was that we are trying to maximize average achievement because doing so enhances economic productivity. But the argument we made for honors classes does not quite say this. Rather it seems to say that we are trying to maximize economic productivity by concentrating resources on those most likely to make professional use of the knowledge they gain. In fact from this perspective, we may not care very much about the learning of other students because they are unlikely to use algebra in their occupations. So it is not obvious that, if we want to maximize economic productivity, we need to maximize average achievement. The achievement of some may have more economic impact than the achievement of others.

So far, the principle of benefit maximizations suggests that we should not admit Teshan into the honors class for two reasons. First, we should not take Teshan's race into account because employing race to confer benefits leads to the inefficient use of educational resources. It does not maximize the gains we should get from their use. Second, if we admit Teshan, we may not admit someone else of higher ability who could make better use of the resources, and we may reduce the value of the class to other students. In short, that Teshan is African American should not count. That he is less able than others to profit from instruction does count.

The principle of benefit maximization does not easily allow us to argue that admitting Teshan is a matter of compensatory justice. The principle of benefit maximization is future oriented because it is consequence oriented and the consequences of our actions occur in the future. Perhaps it is true that the fact that Teshan is less able to profit from instruction results from the inferior education often provided to African Americans, but this is irrelevant to future consequences. What is relevant is that he is now less able to profit from instruction. When reasoning from the principle of benefit maximization, the past is morally dead. It is the future that counts.

Making efficiency and ability to profit central also makes a case against providing additional resources for Susan. Advocates for disabled students often make efficiency arguments for providing educational resources for them. It is often claimed, for example, that by educating disabled students we make it possible for them to be productively employed rather than being permanently dependent. But, as an appeal to economic efficiency, this is a dangerous line of argument for two reasons. First, there are some disabled students for whom this is not true. Consider students with severe cognitive disabilities. By providing an appropriate education for them, we may enhance the quality and dignity of their lives, but we may never make them self sufficient or employable. Does it follow that, in such cases, disabled students should be denied an education entirely? Second, what the principle of benefit maximization requires is that we make the most efficient use of our resources. Even if providing more resources for disabled students does make it more likely that they will become self sufficient, it does not follow that this is the most efficient use of educational resources.

The case of students with significant disabilities can be viewed as a special case of the tendency of the principle of benefit maximization to concentrate resources on high ability rather than on high needs students. If we are trying to maximize achievement or if we are trying to maximize economic productivity, we may get little benefit from educating very hard to educate children. Special education, from this perspective, often turns out to be an inefficient use of resources. If we come to this rather harsh conclusion, it should lead us to reconsider the assumptions that led us here.

Of course Susan is not severely cognitively disabled. She is blind. However, her education will cost more, and if we are interested in maximizing achievement or economic productivity there may well be other more efficient uses for our resources. Again, this should lead us to suspect our assumptions.

When we first discussed utilitarianism and the principle of benefit maximization we pointed out that we were skeptical about it because sometimes it seemed to justify abhorrent conclusions. The example we used was that benefit maximization might justify torturing someone for entertainment if doing so gave the torturers more pleasure than it cause their victim pain. This example and the educational examples we have been discussing are both examples of a particular flaw with the principle of benefit maximization. The flaw is that in trying to maximize some outcome, it is attentive only to the average quantity of that outcome, but not its distribution. Thus it is capable of justifying significant deprivations or significant suffering so long as the decisions that produce these deprivations or sufferings result in the improvement of the average.

This objection can be expressed as a simple point. When we are considering questions of distributive justice, we do need to consider the consequences of our actions, but we also need to consider how they affect each individual. Policies that impose significant harm on some are not justified even if they result in the maximization of some benefit. This is not to say that efficiency does not count or that we should not consider who is able to make the best use of educational resources. It is to say that this is not all that counts.

How might we think about these issues from a nonconsequentialist point of view? The starting point must be the idea of respect for persons. We can consider how nonconsequentialists might think about our two cases, by considering two of the objections we made to the principle of benefit maximization above.

First, nonconsequentialist views allow us to take history into account. While the future counts, so does the past. We may argue that respecting the dignity and worth of each person allows us, perhaps requires us, to set right the injustices that have been done to others insofar as we are able. Restoring people to the position they would have enjoyed had they not be victims of an injustice is one way to show that we fully value them. Equal respect for persons has room for compensatory justice.

This does not decide the matter. Our case does not claim that Teshan was done an injustice as an individual. While African Americans may still suffer racism as a group, we have not claimed that Teshan has been the victim of racial discrimination or that this discrimination was the cause of his performance in mathematics. It rather suggests that Teshan may have been disadvantaged as a member of a group, and the roots of this injustice may be historical. Teshan may have been disadvantaged because of the long term consequences of American racism, not because of some particular act of discrimination against him. Does this warrant compensatory justice? The idea that we should view Teshan as entitled to compensatory justice requires discussion of these issues and more. What we do claim is that a nonconsequentialist approach puts these issues on the table because it warrants compensatory justice.

A second criticism of the principle of benefit maximization is that it warrants unfair trades. When we discussed why we should take the ability to profit from instruction into account in allocating resources, we suggested that one reason why we should do so is that expending resources on those most able to make good use of them benefits everyone. But we went on to notice that benefit maximization does not actually require this and its application often does not result in this. What benefit maximization requires is that we adopt the distribution of resources that produces the highest average. This is consistent with trades between the welfare of some and the welfare of others. Indeed, it is consistent with trades that are quite damaging to some.

Suppose we want to take the idea that we should adopt a particular distribution of resources only when it actually does make everyone better off. What might this mean? One answer to this question can be constructed by adapting an idea taken from the philosopher John Rawls.[8] (Our use of his views takes some liberties.) Rawls has suggested a principle that is intended as an answer to the question concerning the kinds of inequalities that can be permitted in a just society. His position is that inequality is permissible when it is to the advantage of everyone. We decide what is to the advantage of everyone by looking at how the distribution affects the welfare of those receiving the lesser share. Justice, says Rawls, requires distributions to be to the advantage of the least advantaged. We must judge inequality from the perspective of the person who is the least well off. If an inequality is to the benefit of the person receiving the lesser share, then it is permissible. Otherwise it is not.

Such a principle might be argued for by appealing to the idea of equal respect for persons. How do we decide if we have shown equal respect for the value of each individual? We do so by being able to show that the least well off people in our society are as well off as they can be. Any inequalities that exist must be shown to generate benefits for all in which even the least advantaged share. As some economists put it, we must maximize the social minimum.

Let's apply this idea to the question of whether it is permissible to have an honors algebra class of the sort that characterizes the program at Roosevelt. We might pose the issue this way: Suppose there was no honors class. All students took algebra and all were taught in the same way. But now we are considering creating an honors class. Those who want this class claim that everyone is better off. If we are to judge this proposal by looking to the welfare of the least advantaged, then we need to show that those who are not selected for the honors program are better off because of its existence. Is this likely?

Here are two reasons why it is possible. First, those students who are not chosen for the honors class might be given instruction more appropriate to their abilities. If so, they might actually learn more. Thus, if we emphasize the goal of increasing achievement, this program might improve the achievement of all students. This is one of the more common argu-

---

8. John Rawls, *A Theory of Justice* (Cambridge, Mass.: Harvard University Press, 1971).

ments for tracking. Second, if we have the honors program those who are enrolled in it might have their prospects for college improved, they might increase the supply of scientists and engineers and might create products and jobs that improved the prospects of those not admitted to the program. *If* these facts are correct, then the existence of the honors program is consistent with the test that we should look at the consequences for the least advantaged.

Why is this a nonconsequentialist view? After all it makes decisions by looking at their consequences. The answer is that while we do need to look at consequences to decide what distribution is to everyone's advantage, the rule itself does not seek to maximize anything. What it seeks is that we show equal respect for the dignity and worth of all. We do this, the argument claims, by seeking policies and practices that treat people as individuals rather than as ciphers in calculating an average. When we permit trades that improve the average welfare at the expense of the welfare of some, we treat those disadvantaged individuals as means to the welfare of others. When we emphasize the welfare of the least advantaged we show respect for all.

Does this give us a reason to admit Teshan to the honors class? Most likely it gives us a reason not to have honors algebra – or at least not to have it in the way it is practiced at Roosevelt. As it is practiced at Roosevelt, its function seems to be to "liberate" the able few from the burden of their less well prepared classmates. It does not seem to seek to teach these students well. Given this, we believe that the program itself, as it currently operates, is unjustified.

If we assume that the program will continue as is, then we should ask how admitting Teshan will affect his education and the education of other students. The same arguments that suggest that Teshan's presence in the honors class may make the class less effective for other students also suggest that if he is assigned to a non-honors class his presence will make that class better. Students learn from other students. If Teshan is more able than the other students in his class, he may improve the class.

If we doubt that Teshan's presence in either class will make a noticeable difference in the class, then this counts as a reason for admitting him to the honors class. We can make him better off without harming anyone else. If all else is equal (which it may not be), we should do this.

If we apply these arguments to disabled students, they suggest a case for providing Susan the resources she needs to effectively learn in her class even if they are extensive. If time is a scarce resource, then Ms. Teal is justified in spending more of her time with Susan than with other students, perhaps even a lot more time. Why? Recall the difficulty with the idea that we want to maximize average achievement. This view threatens to sharply reduce the resources we committed to high needs students since those resources could purchase more learning if we committed them to the learning of other students. But such a view fails to respect the equal worth of disabled students. Their learning is sacrificed to that of more able (or more cheaply educated) students.

This suggests that in the classroom often the students we should view as least advantaged are high needs students such as Susan. We should, thus, be willing to provide more resources to such students. We show equal respect for all by showing that we value the weakest among us.

There is one more line of argument to consider. In our consideration of *Brown* we suggested that we could consider *Brown* in two different ways. We said that we could look at it as asserting a doctrine of equality of educational opportunity. All students deserve an equal chance to succeed. But we could also view *Brown* as asserting a view about democratic community. In democratic communities, all deserve equal respect and all are equally valued. Thus it is illegitimate to act in such a way that we express contempt or devalue some individuals in our society.

This argument suggests two things. First, it suggests that we can evaluate social institutions and their results *expressively*. In a sense social institutions speak to us. When we find that the more desirable positions in society systematically have fewer members of minority groups that expresses the idea that we value those who are under represented less than others. When we look at a classroom and we find that disabled students are not there or that are they are effectively excluded by how the class is conducted, this expresses the idea that they are less valuable and less valued than others. In contrast, when we find reasonably proportionate representation of poor and minority students in our institutions and when disabled people are included as much as is possible, this expresses a commitment to the equality and dignity of all.

Second, the idea that we judge institutions by what they express is a nonconsequentialist position. It judges inclusion or exclusion by the criteria of equal respect and consistency. When we consider how minorities or disable people should be treated, we should see ourselves as minorities or disabled. What treatment would we want?

These arguments do not ignore the importance of ability to profit. Sometimes we do wish to focus resources on those who are most able. What it does is to help us to see the relevance of ability to profit in a different context than one that emphasizes maximization of achievement or economic productivity. It suggests that we judge inclusion and exclusion by three criteria.

First, under most circumstances we should not make decisions based on race or other factors in the list in the NEA Code. We may, however, consider such factors in order to remedy prior injustices.

Second, we may consider ability to profit, but we must do so in a way that is not disadvantageous to high needs students. We need to distribute resources in ways that benefit everyone. Often a useful criterion is to see if our decisions improve the welfare of the least advantaged among us.

Finally, we should look at our communities from the perspective of what commitments they express. Do they express a commitment to the equal value and dignity of all, or do they express privilege and exclusion?

## REFLECTIONS ON METHOD

Notice several things about the arguments we have made here. First, we think that it is important to note that both consequentialist and nonconsequentialist theories can give reasons why we should value equality of opportunity. They differ in that they provide different justifications for the idea. We have constructed cases designed to highlight the differences between these different ways of thinking because we think that this is pedagogically useful. At the same time, we think it important to notice that most moral theories tend to give similar answers to many basic moral questions. Indeed, we would be unlikely to accept them if they did not. After all, we have argued that ethical inquiry begins with our moral intuitions. What we are trying to do in hard cases is to establish a kind of reflective equilibrium by discovering moral principles that preserve our basic intuitions while giving grounds for them and explaining why we must reject some intuitions that seemed initially plausible.

It follows that conflicting moral theories are of most use in understanding hard cases. It is hard cases where we need to inquire deeply into the justification of core principles. But you should not conclude from our numerous hard cases that we think that moral agreement is rare and difficult. In fact most human beings think that murder, theft, and lying are wrong. They do not need an ethical theory to know this. It is hard cases that require theorizing.

Second, it is important to notice the complex interaction between facts and moral principles in our discussions. This is true even for nonconsequentialist theories. These theories judge consequence by criteria such as respect for persons and consistency, rather than by what maximizes some benefit, but we still cannot apply them to the world without facts.

Perhaps these comments and the discussions of this section will seem to blur the distinction between consequentialist and nonconsequentialist theories. We think this is a good thing. In making this distinction we do want you to notice that different ethical theories bring different criteria to bear in judging facts, but we have not wanted to communicate the idea that ethical judgments can be made in the absence of facts.

## ADDITIONAL CASES

### Equal but Separate

Deerpark School of Sylvan is part of the new Madison County Consolidated School District, a planned realignment of educational facilities and government. The new system combines under a central county administration the old schools of Jefferson City, which have been dominated by minorities and the urban poor in recent years, with the modern schools of the richer suburbs. This plan was developed as a result of pressure from Jefferson City residents and federal attorneys in order to guarantee educational parity and an acceptable racial balance in the area schools. It also provides additional revenue and improved services for the city schools. Under this plan, many students from Jefferson City now attend schools in surrounding towns like Sylvan.

Some teachers have followed these students to their new schools, as part of a limited reassignment of faculty in the new county system. Rosemary Anderson, a fourth-grade instructor, is among this group. Rosemary had come to Jefferson City with the Teachers Corps ten years ago, and she had remained with the city school system afterwards. Her years in these schools had been full of struggle and happiness. She and her fellow teachers had worked hard to provide a decent education for disadvantaged children, using meager resources, determination, and imagination. Rosemary was a bit sad that a period of educational experimentation in Jefferson City had ended, but she believed that the new system would be best for the students in the long run. Her decision to transfer to Deerpark School was based, in part, upon a desire to follow the progress of the Jefferson City children in the new program.

Upon arriving in her new classroom on the first day of school, Rosemary has discovered that she has followed these children much more closely than she had expected. Most of the children in her classroom are from Jefferson City. After consultation with another teacher, Rosemary has found that all of the students in the other fourth-grade class are from the Sylvan area. In her opinion, this state of affairs does not accord with the spirit and intent of the agreement that created the unified county school district. The present arrangement at Deerpark School will only perpetuate de facto racial and economic segregation and minimize the desirable educational objectives that the consolidation plan was designed to encourage. The children in her classroom will have little personal contact with the other students and will remain strangers, possibly antagonists, to the children of Sylvan. Deerpark School seems to have abandoned any official responsibility to direct the racial and cultural interaction that might serve to ameliorate the cleavages that afflict life in Madison County. This will only serve to harm the interests of both groups of children. In a very real sense, the school is an educational failure. It is undemocratic in its practices, and it is not really desegregated. Rosemary Anderson has decided to confront the principal on this matter.

Robert Shire, the principal of Deerpark School and a resident of Sylvan, has attempted to assuage Rosemary's anger and has explained the present placement policy at the school. Deerpark School and the people of Sylvan will comply with the provisions of the consolidation plan, but they also intend to preserve the educational quality of the school. Over the years, Deerpark School has developed a very progressive, unified curriculum and has been very successful in its educational mission. The Jefferson City children will need time to adjust to the new curriculum. Also, the students from the city are not as educationally advanced as their new peers, and the standardized test scores for reading and mathematics show this. It will take time to bring their performances up to the proper grade level. Under these circumstances, Mr. Shire believes that it would be disruptive to instruction and unfair to both groups of children if they are thrown together with no regard for educational attainments. Mr. Shire has asked Rosemary to have patience with the present situation.

*Some Questions*

1.  Is this a case of differences that make a difference? Should the Jefferson City children be treated differently because their reading and math scores are low?
2.  Clearly this is a case of legally imposed desegregation that may meet the letter, but not the spirit and purpose, of the new arrangements. Is this a case where what is legal and what is ethical can be meaningfully separate questions? Which should take precedence here?
3.  Imagine you are Rosemary. Construct an argument using appropriate ethical principles and ideas that you would present to Mr. Shire and take further, to the board perhaps, if you failed to convince him of your position.
4.  We have said that facts enter into ethical reasoning in important ways. Could you alter the facts of this case in a way that justifies the continued de facto segregation of the Jefferson City children?

## Inclusive?

Last Thursday Dmitri Karpov had been visited after school by two of his students, Sean O'Malley and Juana Frank. They had said that they represented Hanover High's local LGBT club. It seemed that next week the club was sponsoring an event that focused on the bullying of LGBT students. Sean and Juana wanted to make an announcement in his social studies class. The announcement would say two things. First, it would ask the students to help end the bullying of LGBT students. Students would be asked to wear a button with a simple message that read "End the Bullying." Second, students would be asked to attend a meeting of the LGBT club where the issue of bullying would be discussed.

The students clearly recognized that what they wanted could be viewed as controversial by some. They were well prepared. They had a written statement that described what they wanted to do in bulleted points. It said among other things that their goals were to deter bullying and to secure tolerance for LGBT students. Nothing, the statement said, would be discussed or advocated that was not concerned with the problem of bullying. No one would seek to recruit new members for the LGBT club or to advocate a homosexual life style. The focus was on bullying. Could they, Juana asked, please have five minutes of class time to ask students to wear buttons and to come to the meeting?

Mr. Karpov went through a quick mental check list. Was LGBT a legitimate school club? Yes. It was on an official list along with other advocacy groups that included Young Republicans, Young Democrats, and the Christian Club. Was the message that Juana and Sean wanted to convey legitimate and appropriate? Mr. Karpov thought it was. There had been issues at Hanover about bullying and gay students had been bullied. He did not see how any reasonable person could object to a message against bullying. And the LGBT students had been careful to note that their agenda for his class and for the meeting was limited to the issue of bullying. His only real doubt was that he wasn't sure that he should give class time for an announcement. After all, Hanover had a lot of groups who might want to announce a lot of events in classes. He did not want his class to become the equivalent of a bulletin board.

Finally, however, he agreed. After all, he was a Civics teacher and the class was Civics. Isn't this democracy in action? He thought that he would make it a policy that students who belonged to advocacy clubs could announce the occasional special event in his class so long as there was no more than one a week. He would tell students this before giving the floor to Juana and Sean. They could make their announcement next Wednesday he said.

When next Wednesday arrived Mr. Karpov quickly regretted his decision. In the back row of his class three students wore complementary sweat shirts. The first read "God Condemns Homosexuality." The second read "Gays can be Cured." The third read "Free Speech for Christians." Mr. Karpov decided to ignore them. Another mistake. When Juana and Sean stood up to make their announcement, they quickly noticed and were obviously stunned. Juana stammered out her part of the announcement. It was all the Sean could do to not break out into tears.

Mr. Karpov decided that it was not fair to Juana and Sean to continue to subject them to what he had belatedly come to see as a kind of harassment. He asked the three students with the offending sweat shirts to come out with him into the hall. There he asked them to please remove the sweat shirts. They refused. In fact one of the students, Peter DeCosta, announced that they would want to take advantage of Mr. Karpov's new policy. The Christian Club would be sponsoring a presentation entitled "The Christian view of Homosexuality" next week, and they wanted to announce it in his class.

Mr. Karpov rather doubted that there was any such thing as *the* Christian view of homosexuality. It seemed to him that religious people were quite divided on the matter. But he decided that it was not going to help to engage these students in a theological debate. Thus, Mr. Karpov marched the three students off to the principal's office. He explained what had happened to Ms. Fletcher, the principal, who had a kind of wry "gee thanks for bringing me this" expression on her face. She did, however, back him up. She explained to the students that while she was sure that they were sincere in their convictions, that she thought they were coura-geous to be willing to express them as they had done, and that she was sure that they did not want to injure anyone, nevertheless, their views were hurtful to LGBT students and thus she would have to ask them to remove the sweat shirts. They again refused and again requested time to announce the topic for the next meeting of the Christian Club.

Ms. Fletcher told them that she was going to assign them to study hall until they took off the sweat shirts, and she took them to an empty confer-ence room where they spent the rest of the day. Mr. Karpov went back to his class and tried to get on with his lesson.

The next day during his open period Mr. Karpov was called to Ms Fletcher's office. The three students were there still wearing the offending sweat shirts. They were accompanied by two of their parents and an attor-ney, Mr. Wong. Mr. Wong said that he was representing the three students and that he was associated with a group named Citizens for Free Speech. He laid out his case: "This issue, Mr. Karpov and Ms Fletcher, is a free speech issue. You have offered classroom time to permit an advocacy group to present its views. You must offer time to those with other views. Moreover, the fact that their views are rooted in religion makes no differ-ence. Religious ideas are still ideas. You cannot give a forum to those who wish to advocate the homosexual agenda and whose ideas are opposed to the Judeo-Christian tradition and not permit religious people to rebut them. The law is quite clear on these matters. "

Mr. Karpov wasn't convinced. He really had no interest in having his classroom turned into a debating society about the hot button issues of the day, including gay rights. His interest was in creating an inclusive class-room. LGBT students often seemed silenced if not downright intimidated by the treatment they received from some other students. He was tempted to ask the attorney what Christian teachings justified bullying LGBT students. Moreover, he had not offered his classroom to the LGBT students to advocate any homosexual agenda. He had offered it to them to invite people to a meeting to discuss bullying. It seemed to him that ending bullying was an essential part of creating an inclusive school. Debating the homo-sexual agenda—and he also doubted there was anything that could be called *the* homosexual agenda—was not.

He was about to say this to Mr. Wong when Ms. Fletcher said, "I doubt that the law is a clear as you suggest, Mr. Wong. Before we continue this conversation I will have to consult the school district's attorney." She gave Mr. Karpov a look that said, "Please shut up" about as loudly as a glance could say anything. He did. But as he left another thought occurred: "If the school is trying to be inclusive by protecting the rights of LGBT students, can it also find a way to include students whose religious convictions are opposed to homosexuality?"

*Some Questions:*

1. We have argued in this chapter that a democratic school is one in which all are equally valued and that this is what we called an expressive right. The school's institutions and practices must express inclusion. How should schools express inclusion of LGTB students? Does helping to oppose bullying express inclusion? How can a school also include those whose religious convictions are opposed to homosexuality?
2. In our discussion of intellectual liberty we suggested that intellectual liberty serves important educational and civic purposes and that it follows that people must be allowed to advocate for unpopular positions. We also suggested that in schools educators have some rights to manage student freedom of expression for educational purposes. Does the idea that free speech requires us to tolerate unpopular ideas extend to hurtful ideas? Is inclusion an educational purpose that might justify a school in restricting the rights of freedom of expression of those who might say hurtful things? Are the messages on the sweat shirts of the three students a form of hate speech? Could they be viewed as bullying?
3. Mr. Karpov and Ms Fletcher view this issue as concerned with inclusion. Mr. Wong views it as about free speech. Who is right?
4. We could have put this case at the end of Chapter 3 or Chapter 5. We put it here because we wanted to expand the range of issues involved in creating democratic community. Does the fact that we could have put it in other places tell us anything about the nature of hard cases?

## FOR FURTHER INQUIRY

Brighouse, Harry. "Educational Equality and Justice." In *A Companion to the Philosophy of Education* edited by Randall Curren. Oxford: Blackwell, 2003.
A discussion of equality of educational opportunity.

*Brown* v. *Board of Education* 347 U.S. 483.
The Supreme Court case that declared segregated schools to be unconstitutional.

The Civil Rights Project. http://www.civilrightsproject.ucla.edu/
A good resource for research on inequality in education.

Fischer, Louis, David Schimmel, and Leslie R. Stellman. *Teachers and the Law.* 6 ed. Boston: Allyn and Bacon, 2003. Chapters 14–16
A good resource for the law on racial inequality and the rights of the disabled.

*Board of Education* v. *Rowley* 458 U. S. 176
The lead Supreme Court case on the rights of the disabled.

Howe, Kenneth R., and Miramontes, Ofelia. *The Ethics of Special Education.* New York: Teachers College Press, 1992.
A discussion of the ethical issues that arise in the context of special education.

Kittay, Eva Feder. *Love's Labor.* New York: Routledge, 1999.
A discussion of dependency and justice with special relevance to the ethics of special education.

Landenson, Robert F. "Inclusion and Justice in Special Education." In *A Companion to the Philosophy of Education,* edited by Randall Curren, 525–39. Oxford: Blackwell, 2003.
A discussion of the inclusion of disabled students.

*Parents Involved in Community Schools* v. *Seattle School Dist. No. 1*
In this case the Supreme Court held that voluntary desegregation plans that use race to assign pupils are unconstitutional.

Rawls, John. *Justice as Fairness: A Restatement.* Cambridge, Massachusetts: Harvard University Press, 2001.
Rawls is the most important American political philosopher of the second half of the 20th century. This is the final version of his theory of justice.

Strike, Kenneth. "Toward a Moral Theory of Desegregation." In *Philosophy and Education: Eightieth Yearbook of the National Society for the Study of Education,* edited by Jonas Soltis, 213–35. Chicago: University of Chicago Press, 1981.
This is a discussion of the moral ideals implicit in major Supreme Court cases.

# Chapter 5

# Diversity: Multiculturalism and Religion

## TWO CASES TO CONSIDER

### Old Earth and the Creation

Paul Huxley is the teacher of AP Biology for the Old Earth Public Schools. Old Earth is an affluent school district with numerous intellectually able students. Many of these students see the AP courses offered by Old Earth as gateways to prestigious universities and good jobs.

Paul Huxley's course contains an extensive unit on natural selection. Paul regards evolution as central to modern biology. He is aware that this unit troubles some of his more religious students who think, for reasons that elude him, that evolution is inconsistent with their belief in God. He is careful not to embarrass these students. Still, he has always noticed that some of them clam up during this unit and a few seem disengaged. Recently, however, this changed. Now he has noted that during the evolution unit some students have begun to talk in an odd way. When they answer questions there is an edge to their voice, and they are careful to describe evolution as "a theory" and to introduce their comments with expressions like "according to evolutionists. . . ." Similar language crops up in homework and on tests. Occasionally Paul even gets an aggressive question. Last week one student asked him how natural selection could explain the evolution of wings, noting that it was impossible according to evolutionary theory for wings to appear all at once and fully developed. Yet half a wing certainly has no survival value. While Paul was not daunted by the question—in fact, he was pleased by the thought it showed—he was puzzled by the change in attitude. Even more puzzling was the fact that those students who suddenly began to use odd expressions and became argumentative also did surprisingly well on the unit. Indeed, sometimes they seemed to know things that he had not taught.

One day he asked a student, Susan Stone, why she insisted on using the kinds of language noted above. Susan was clearly very intimidated by the question, but with a little patience and reassurance, Paul managed to get the story out of her. The drift of the story was this: A local clergyman had organized a seminar on evolution for students from his and other local churches. This seminar coincided with Paul Huxley's unit on evolution and was intended to rebut it. It was taught by a local civil engineer, Carl Bryan, and, if Susan's account was correct, it had managed to enroll five to ten of Paul's students every year. It was devoted to providing students with a Creationist account of human origins and discussing the evidence against evolution. Students were encouraged to learn what Paul taught, but were also taught to describe what they had learned in a language that did not commit them to its truth. Having gotten her courage up, Susan gave Paul Huxley a parting shot that disturbed him greatly. She said, "You know Mr. Huxley, you give us a really biased account. You don't tell us any of the evidence against evolution. But Mr. Bryan does. Why don't you present both sides, and why do you treat Creationists as though they were idiots? What are you afraid of? Anyway, we tell all of the other students what we learn, so now nobody really believes your atheistic lies and nobody feels put down by you anymore."

Paul Huxley thought about this for some time. He wasn't an atheist, and he didn't like being called a liar. He was just teaching his subject. But since his students were learning the material and were doing fine on the AP exam, he wasn't sure that there was really a problem. Finally, he decided that there was a problem. It wasn't just that someone was teaching his students to reject what seemed to him to be the well-documented findings of his field, although that did bother him. It was also that students were getting two conflicting accounts with no opportunity to hear their merits debated. The more he thought about it, the more it offended his idea of a good education. Moreover, he was distressed by Susan's reaction to his teaching. He didn't think he put down anyone. He just told the truth. Did it injure people just to hear an idea that they disagree with? He didn't lie, and he didn't coerce belief. Was it now a crime to tell the truth?

Eventually he went to his principal, Janice Meek, with two questions. First, "I want to deal with this somehow in class; what should I say?" Second, "Could I organize a seminar after school and invite the minister, Carl Bryan, the students, and maybe a few other people to discuss the issues? Maybe we could talk openly about this for a few weeks." Ms. Meek thought Paul should say something in class, but she wasn't sure what. She thought that such a seminar would be about as much fun as sticking your head in a beehive and might be illegal to boot. She was surprised by the school district attorney's opinion that "Since no one has been foolhardy enough to try this, it's hard to know if it's illegal, but I think it could be done in such a way that it would stand up in court." And she did see Paul's point.

## New Harbor and the Iroquois Confederation

Marie Carter is the head of the social studies department of New Harbor High. She has recently been called into the superintendent's office and given an unexpected, but interesting assignment. She is unsure what to do. Here is what Dr. Estabon, the superintendent, said.

> Marie, I've just had a visit from a delegation from the reservation. A Mr. Ken Le France, who headed the delegation and who seems to be some sort of chief, has told me that his students who attend New Harbor are alienated from our program. I'm not even sure that I know what alienated means, but God knows that they sometimes don't do very well. He says that they're tired of attending a school that ignores their culture and destroys their self-esteem and that we need to do something that shows our respect for his culture. He thinks that this will build self-esteem among his people and that Indian students will do better.
>
> Look, maybe he's right. This is a bit beyond my experience. But Le France seems like a good guy. He wasn't belligerent, and he was really concerned about his kids. I don't think we do very well by them. Do you?
>
> Well anyhow, I told him that we'd do something multicultural that discussed Iroquois culture and the Iroquois contribution to the United States. Social studies seems like the place to do it. How would you like to come up with something? You find us something to teach, and I'll make a place in the schedule for it.

New Harbor is a rural school district in upstate New York. It intersects a reservation in which the members of a tribe belonging to the Iroquois Confederation live. The students on the eastern side of the reservation attend New Harbor High School. There are also some other Native Americans who do not live on the reservation who attend. In fact, about 20% of the students in the district claim Iroquois ancestry. Those who come from the reservation tend to be poor. They are often passive in school. They tend to drop out as soon as they are sixteen.

Marie isn't convinced that a unit or two on the Native American culture and contribution to the United States will do much to help. She's not convinced that teaching about Iroquois culture is going to overcome the effects of years of poverty and oppression. Also, since to the best of her knowledge Indians had been the object of much oppression, she wasn't sure that they'd had much of a chance to contribute to U.S. culture, unless one thought that being the object of some degrading movies was a contribution. She is afraid that a close look at some piece of Iroquois history will only make Native American students feel more alienated. Finally, she isn't sure that substituting a discussion of the Iroquois Confederation for some math or English is what's required to advance the prospects of these students. Nevertheless, she wants to give it a try.

As she researches the topic, she is pleasantly surprised to find that recently several scholars have advanced the view that the form of government of the Iroquois Confederation during the Colonial period had a significant influence on the views of those who drafted the U.S. Constitution. Two things seem true about this claim. First, it seems clear that the Iroquois did have a form of government that was broadly democratic in its character. Chiefs were elected. Decision were made in a council that involved much discussion and consensus was emphasized. This model of government continues to be important in how current members of the Iroquois Nation conduct their affairs. Moreover, unlike the U.S. government, where legislators have a hard time looking beyond the next opinion poll, the Iroquois were encouraged to consider the effects of their decisions on seven generations. There are many reasons to commend the Iroquois view of government. Congress could learn a lot from the Iroquois.

Second, while there is some reason to suppose that Ben Franklin and some others who were in attendance at the constitutional convention of 1787 were aware of the governance structure of the Iroquois Confederation, the claim that the Iroquois model of government had a significant influence on the drafting of the U.S. Constitution is hotly contested. While there is evidence for the claim, it has not convinced many skeptical historians. Thus, the truth of the matter remains in dispute. As Marie studies the matter, she comes to the opinion that while the Iroquois system of government has much to commend it, it is unlikely that it had any real influence on the views of the framers. Of course, she is willing to study the Iroquois system of government and to discuss the issue of its contribution to the drafting of the Constitution, but she is not sure that putting the matter on the table as an open issue will provide the kind of cultural affirmation the Iroquois are looking for.

Marie has another difficulty. She has recently had a visit from Carla James, a local physician and, more important, a leading voice on the New Harbor school board. Dr. James was displeased with Marie's plans for a unit on the Iroquois. She viewed it as divisive. In Dr. James' words, "We need to stop telling people how they've been oppressed and how distinct and valuable their culture is, and we need to start to help them think of themselves as Americans. Multiculturalism just continues the alienation, separatism, and economic exclusion of minorities. If we keep it up, pretty soon the Balkanization of America will do for us what it's done for Bosnia."

## DISPUTE

A: One of the great things about our democracy is its pluralism. We have people from all races and religions, from all the countries and cultures of the world. We each learn from the other, and we all live together in peace and harmony.

B: Wait a minute! Our history, even our most recent history, is not full of peace and harmony. It is full of race riots, church burnings, ugly confrontations, marches, bombings, and FBI/ATF raids and sieges. Diversity is the catalyst not of peace but of hatred, discrimination, and the sanctioned use of brute force.

A: Yes, such things happen, but if you think of the country as a whole, these incidents are statistically insignificant. Ninety-nine percent of the population gets along with, or at least is tolerant of, others who are different. Tolerance is our solution to difference.

B: But just acknowledging and recognizing differences will not solve the problem. Ninety-nine percent of the time whites see blacks as different, and inwardly, unconsciously, see themselves as superior. Blacks learn early that they are different and feel a twinge of inferiority when treated in certain ways by whites. The same is true of Jews, born-again Christians, Hispanics, Native Americans, Asians, and numerous other minority groups in our land. Young children pick up signals from their parents and other authority figures as well as from their peers. They learn to feel different by osmosis. We can try to teach tolerance in our schools, but the roots of difference have already grown deep and scar the souls of our children.

A: Very poetic! Yet your very description of the problem hints at its solution. Schools must be an oasis of tolerance, teaching it by example and osmosis. Different cultures need to be studied, and their contributions appreciated. Different religions also have to be explored and understood as different ways human beings define the spiritual realm.

B: Oh, be realistic! There is not enough time to teach about all the cultures in the world. Even if there were, by whose cultural standards of judgment are we to determine what are *worthwhile* contributions? Standards differ in different cultures. Teaching about different religions can be dangerous, too. Are all of them right in some sense? What happens to your own spiritual beliefs when you are asked to appreciate the contrary beliefs of others? Is there no true religion? Doesn't truth count?

A: Truth is not the point here. Tolerance and understanding are. What we need in a pluralistic, multicultural, democratic society is to learn to live peacefully together and respect difference, not tell the truth together.

B: Are you saying that truth is not important in our schools or in our democratic society? I can't believe it!

## CONCEPTS AND ISSUES

Religious diversity and multiculturalism are complex issues. We aren't going to be able to do more than scratch the surface about them. We want to focus on four issues that are present in our cases. First is the issue of alienation and self-identity. Some students are alienated from school because the school seems to reject something about who they are. Some students in Mr. Huxley's class feel that he is hostile to their religion. Some Iroquois students in New Harbor feel that their culture is ignored and disparaged. Second, there is an issue of truth and of who controls it. In one class there is a dispute about human origins. In New Harbor, Marie Carter fears an approach to the topic of the Iroquois influence on the Constitution that treats it as an open and debatable question. She worries that the Iroquois students may feel a personal stake in the claim and that they may experience any questioning of it as personal disparagement. Do schools have a right to teach ideas that are inconsistent with peoples' religious views or that raise questions about the worth or contribution of various cultures? Who gets to decide what schools will view as the truth or what questions are open to debate? Does the school have a right to act on its view of the truth when that seems to cause pain to students? Third is the issue of dialogue. Both Paul and Marie think that controversial issues should be debated. Perhaps they share Mill's view that truth is best sought through free and open debate. Thus they are dissatisfied with situations where students learn one thing in school and another in church or where hard questions are avoided because someone might be offended. But who will set the rules for the discussion, and how will it be made a fair debate? Who owns the truth or the rules of discourse? Finally, there is the question of the one and the many. Should schools work to create a shared American culture? Or should they try to respect each culture equally? If they do the first, will not minorities be oppressed and alienated? If they do the second, will not our society become Balkanized and politically unstable? Is there a middle ground?

We have two purposes to accomplish in this chapter. First, we want to develop some positions about diversity. Second, we want to consider some questions about the adequacy of some of the analytic concepts we have tried to teach you throughout this book. We have developed this book as though it were a debate between two broad theories of ethics, a consequentialist view and a nonconsequentialist view. These are two versions of what we might call the ethics of modernity. Modernity has been challenged by some philosophers who are sometimes called postmodernists. We can't do justice to this complicated debate here, but allow us a brief attempt to characterize it.

Among the things that postmodernists have argued is that in their desire to bring everything under the sway of some grand theory, the philosophies of modernity are insufficiently attentive to difference. Modernists claim that regardless of how different we are, we are all the same in some relevant way and that it is this sameness that is the most important thing about us. We may differ in our views, in our religions, in our ethnicity, in our gender, in our history, but after all of these differences have been noted, we are all persons or utility maximizers (or both).

However, postmodernists claim our differences are more basic than our sameness. Indeed, perhaps our sameness is illusory What, after all, is a person? Does our description of a person actually describe some real feature of every human being that is also central in our ethical lives? Perhaps this entity called a person is just a metaphysical delusion that names nothing. Even worse, perhaps a description of a person is really a characterization of people as European men see them. Perhaps it tries to universalize traits that are European, or male, or white, or Christian, but not universal. If so, then an ethic that treats personhood as central may subtly impose the culture or experience of some on others. Analogously, perhaps the picture of human beings as utility or pleasure maximizers is the view of people conveniently held by capitalist economists. Thus it serves the interest of capitalism. Perhaps we need to stop looking for some characteristic like personhood that is central and shared, and to notice the importance of difference and particularity.

Consider the issue of truth. Many philosophers have argued that people experience the world through the interpretive frameworks they receive through their cultures. We do not all see the world in the same way. Perhaps we live in irreducibly different worlds. Perhaps there is no Truth; there is only the experience of women or men, of European Americans and African Americans and Hispanic Americans, only different truths, only different ways of seeing the world. The only truths we can have are truths that presuppose our background and assume who we are. Thus all truths are partial and perspectival. No truth is the whole truth. Every truth assumes something about the perspective of the individual whose truth it is.

Notice how these ideas connect. The idea that truth is partial and perspectival means that it is unlikely that we will ever achieve any ethical theories that are genuinely universal. We are irreducibly different. All theories assume someone's particular experience. Views that try to see us as persons or as utility maximizers end up imposing someone's truth as everyone's truth. Thus all attempts at ethical generalization are oppressive. They deny who we are, and they impose on us someone else's definition of what we should be.

These are not views we would accept in the form we have stated them here. Yet we do take such claims seriously. First, we think that they pose an important challenge to the way we have proceeded. Thus we think you should have a chance to consider them and that there is something to be learned from them. Second, they provide an important warning to those who try to develop ethical theories. Even if there are some things that can be said about people in general and even if there are some important universal ethical claims that can be defended, we still need to be careful that we do not mistake the views of our culture or our own personal biases for these claims. We need to test any claims carefully. We need to be especially careful to do so when we are dealing with someone with a background that is significantly different from our own. Third, these concerns provide an especially useful window on the questions of pluralism and diversity that teachers must face in schools.

Here is how we are going to proceed. First, we are going to describe a view of religious and cultural diversity that emphasizes the themes of alienation, difference, and the perspectival nature of truth. We will then contrast this view with views of diversity developed from a nonconsequentialist and then a consequentialist perspective. We will then make a few comments on the strengths and weaknesses of each.

## RADICAL PLURALISM

Are Americans one people? Should they be? Do schools have any obligation to take many and make them one? *E pluribus Unum?* In years past many educators thought they had such an obligation. It was the job of the school to Americanize immigrants. People with diverse languages, religions, and customs were to pass through the school and be made Americans by being stirred into the melting pot. Not only was diversity not valued, it was to be eliminated in the name of creating a new kind of person, an American.

Of course, Americans have respected some kinds of diversity The Bill of Rights included two phrases, usually called the Establishment and Free Exercise Clauses, that say "Congress shall make no law effecting an establishment of religion nor prohibiting the free exercise thereof." However, even religious tolerance was limited in practice. Until the 1960s many states required the school day to begin with readings from the Protestant Bible and with the Lord's Prayer. Religious toleration often applied only to different kinds of Protestants. Indeed, in nineteenth-century America, Catholics found public schools sufficiently unfriendly that they began their own school system.

Other kinds of diversity were not respected. Africans were enslaved. Native Americans were driven west, persecuted sometimes to extinction, and confined to reservations. Few minorities or immigrant populations have found America respectful of their culture, religion, or ethnicity. Some have found it viciously repressive and exploitative.

Public schools have tried hard to make us one or to behave as though we were already one, and that one was often Protestant, *white,* and Northern European. Others were to be remade into this model or to accommodate to it, or they were simply excluded.

Is this wrong? If so, why? The first answer we will explore emphasizes the importance of people's religion, culture, or ethnicity to their sense of identity and views the failure to respect their religion, culture, or ethnicity as a form of violence against this socially constructed self.[9]

In our cases, the school has denied or failed to affirm something important to some students, their religion, or their culture. But what's this got to do with who these students are, with their identity? One response is that people's religion, culture, and ethnicity are not just facts about them, but are central to their self-understanding. Susan Stone is a student' at Old Earth, and she is a Christian. The first thing is just a fact about her; the second is a part of who she is. If she had to transfer to another school, she would just be Susan Stone in a different school. But if she were no longer a Christian, she would be a fundamentally different person. Her religion is part of who she is. This may also be true of many Iroquois students as well. That they are Iroquois is not just a contingent fact about them: It is part of who they are. Their ethnicity or culture defines them.

If so, then one reason that can be given for respecting diversity is that to fail to do so is to fail to affirm—or even to reject—who people are. It is to deny their worth. Thus, it does an especially insidious kind of violence to them.

Trying to respect diversity raises questions of truth what is to count as truth, and who is to control what is to count as true. In the Old Earth school district the alleged failure to respect religious diversity consists in teaching evolution, a theory that some Americans feel is inconsistent with their religious beliefs. If religion is central to the identity of some people

---

9. This account owes much to Charles Taylor, "The Politics of Recognition," in A. Gutmann (Ed.), *Multiculturalism: Examining the Politics of Recognition* (Princeton, NJ: Princeton University Press, 1994); however, we have made no effort to be faithful to the details of his account.

in Mr. Huxley's class, then teaching evolution may be experienced by these students as a kind of self-rejection. Mr. Huxley has not just taught them something they happen not to believe, he has denied something that is essential to who they are.

Similarly, it may be important to various cultures in the United States to discuss their culture and history and to teach their contributions to the nation. When Iroquois students see the value of their culture acknowledged and find that their people have made an important contribution to the founding document of the nation, they may feel affirmed. If they define themselves as Iroquois, then discovering that the Iroquois have a valuable culture and have done something significant for the nation might be expected to enhance their sense of self-worth.

But what if the claims about the Iroquois contribution to the drafting of the Constitution are not true? Should the Iroquois students feet diminished on that account? If they identify themselves as Iroquois, should they suffer a loss of self-worth if they find that the Iroquois did not in fact make this contribution? Perhaps it is a mistake to link one's sense of self-worth to claims about cultural values or historical facts that may not stand up to examination. Are all cultures equal? Has every culture made some important contribution to ours? (And why must it be to ours?) If not, are their members unequal on that account? If we believe that all people should be valued equally, must we also hold that all cultures are of equal value? How would we know that?

And how should the schools or the teachers feel about these two cases? Do people have a right to equal dignity? Does the school have a right to teach ideas such as evolution or to question the historical contribution of various groups if the sense of equal worth is diminished thereby? In thinking about this question, it is useful to consider that it may be the history of the majority in a society that is most likely to assert self-affirming myths. Everyone wants their group affirmed, but majorities often have the power to enforce self-affirmation.

There are a number of things to notice about this. One is that this line of reasoning provides a powerful incentive to take two additional steps. As we have described the issue, we have developed it as though there might be a conflict between some people's sense of self-worth and the (possible) truth about their religion, culture, or history. Must schools lie or hide the truth in order to affirm the equal worth of their students? This formulation seems intolerable.

But we might avoid the dilemma if we could also assert two other ideas. First, let us suppose that truth is relative either to central theoretical assumptions or to culture. Second, let us assume that people have a right to control their own truth.

Let's see how this might work out for Creationism and evolution. Religious people who reject evolution (and many do not) sometimes argue in the following way. They claim that much of the so-called evidence for the great age of the universe and for evolution is question-begging. It assumes that God does not exist. Consider, for example, an argument for the great age of the universe. If we are to believe what scientists tell us about the vast size of the universe and about the speed of light, then it seems that we can see objects that are so distant that their light must have been traveling for millions or billions of years to reach us. If so, then the universe must be more than a few thousand years old, as some Creationists claim.

Creationists have responded that when God created the universe He may have created the light from these distant stars and galaxies as light already in transit. The evolutionist's argument for the age of the universe assumes a universe without God. Thus the argument for the great age of the universe fails unless we already assume that it was not created by God.

Sometimes Creationists will generalize this argument. If we believe in God and that the universe and life are His creation, we can easily interpret all of the supposed evidence for evolution so as to be consistent with this belief. Evolutionists only see a universe in which chance and natural selection reign because they have already denied the possibility of God. But where evolutionists see chance and natural selection, Creationists can see purpose and design. Everything depends on the assumptions with which we start.

Then the next move: If truth is relative to our starting point, why should the starting point of the evolutionist count for more than the starting point of the Creationist? What gives the evolutionist the right to try to dominate the minds of the children of Creationists? If this right is not grounded in the possession of the real Truth in the matter—and it has been shown that it cannot be—then it is nothing more than arbitrary power. By what right do evolutionists compel people of faith to send their children to public schools where they have a monopoly on what is to count as truth? Do not Creationists have the right to control their own truth?

The Iroquois may make similar arguments. They might argue that historical truth is a matter of interpretation, that they have the right to their own interpretation, and that they have the right to the final say about what picture of the Iroquois is presented in schools.

There is an even more interesting (we think) version of this argument possible here. Why should the Iroquois be so concerned to show that they have made a contribution to the drafting of the U.S. Constitution? This assumes the importance of the Constitution. But why should the Iroquois, people who have been oppressed by the white man and by the United States government, be so eager to have contributed to the white man's Constitution? Do they need to impress the white man that they have been important to something he values? Perhaps what the Iroquois need to discover and to control are standards of value that come from their own culture.

If we generalize this argument, the result is the following: Every culture has its own standards of value and of truth that are central to it. These standards are right for that culture. Since there is no general Truth about them, then one culture may not reasonably impose its standards of worth on another. Every culture owns its own standards.

These arguments (if we accept them) tend to secure the dignity and worth of individuals by rendering their religion or their culture unassailable, by viewing all cultures as equally valuable, and by asserting as a general rule that every religion or culture owns its own truth. Along the way, it also leads to a radical pluralism. Societies are viewed as constituted primarily by difference and by groups characterized by their differences. There can be no question of subjecting one culture to another's truth. Difference rules.

## OTHER DEFENSES OF DIVERSITY

Now we want to look at how nonconsequentialsts and consequentialists might look at religious or cultural diversity.

A nonconsequentialist might reason about diversity as follows: The fact that is most important about people is not their ethnic identity or their religion, but their personhood. It is their status as persons, as moral agents, that is the basis of equal rights and of the respect we must show them.

However, if we are to respect people as moral agents, we must respect their choices. We cannot compel them to adopt our religion or our view of a good life, or our view of a worthy culture, even if we think we are right and they are wrong. We owe equal respect to different religions or cultures, not because they are equally true or equally valuable, but because they have been chosen by people who have equal rights. (Here we are expanding an argument we made in Chapters 3 and 4.)

Notice some features of this view. First, since rights are rooted in personhood and rights are enforceable, we do not have to tolerate everything in schools. We do not have to tolerate racism, for example. We may promote racial (or religious or ethnic) tolerance in schools, and we may prevent people from acting on their racism. What nonconsequentialists often say here is that people have a duty to be just, but that they are also entitled to have and to pursue their own concept of a good life. It is this self-chosen sense of the good, which includes religion and culture, that we must respect even if we disagree or believe that ours is superior.

Thus nonconsequentialists do have a plausible approach to explaining what it is that people should have in common and how they may permissibly differ. Everyone should be just, and we may seek and enforce a shared view of justice. But we may not seek to regulate people's views of a good life. May we use the schools to make people Americans? Yes, if we mean that we may try to use schools to teach the essentials of a just constitution and to promote a common political culture based on it. No, if that means that we can use schools to promote a shared religion, a common culture, or a shared identity beyond the political culture warranted by a just constitution.

This view does not root tolerance or pluralism in cultural relativism. We must tolerate other people's religions even if we are sure they are false and ours true. We must respect other people's culture even if we are convinced that ours is superior. What we are respecting is the right to choose, not the adequacy of the choice.

Consider how this might work out in Mr. Huxley's biology class. Mr. Huxley does have a duty to respect the religious views of his students even when they involve Creationism, a view that he regards as silly and benighted. But respecting Creationism does not require Mr. Huxley to hold that Creationism is somehow true for Creationists. (Nor must Creationists believe that evolution is true for Mr. Huxley.) What it does require him to do is to respect the students' right to their own views. This might mean, for example, that he has to carefully distinguish between asking his students to know what evolution is as a framework in biology, and asking them to believe it. He must word exam questions so that students can answer them honestly without affirming a belief in evolution. He must not grade down for rejecting evolution. But he does not have to be a relativist about evolution. Tolerance does not trump truth.

Also, in teaching tolerance, schools would need to be careful to help students to understand that they need to tolerate views and life styles even if they disapprove of them. But they would also have to respect students' right to disapproval. For example, schools might explain to students whose religion holds that homosexuality is a sin that homosexuals nevertheless are entitled to equal rights. But schools should not require that these students view homosexuality as merely an alternative life style.

Respecting diverse cultures probably should be viewed as requiring that schools reflect the diversity of American cultures in their teaching. Thus, they might well find it important to teach about the Iroquois culture in schools with a significant Iroquois population or in all schools. However, schools need not falsify or invent history in order to present a favorable view of every culture. Nor do they need to treat every aspect of every culture with approval. And this may be an especially important point about the culture of the majority. Schools owe their first obligation to the truth when they can find it. (We do not profess to know what the truth about the Iroquois Confederation and the Constitution is.) While truth may be difficult to come up with, it is not relative, at least not in the form described above, and cultures do not own their own truth. Nonconsequentialists can acknowledge that people may feel injured when they have to face something unpleasant about their history or their culture, and since this is a real harm, they should avoid causing such harm unnecessarily. But they can also argue that causing people this kind of injury is not the same as rejecting their worth as human beings. People's self-worth should depend on the fact that they are persons and moral agents, not on the truth of their religions or the achievements of their culture.

A nonconsequentialist might also note that the radical pluralist argument described above may be inconsistent with asking white people to own up to and to rectify their oppression of minorities. After all, if truth is relative and if people own their own truth, why may not white people invent a history to their own liking? Arguably much of the history once taught (perhaps still taught) in public schools was written to support and justify white domination or white superiority and to minimize the fact of white oppression. Slavery has often been represented as benevolent paternalism. Was it? If white people choose to think so, isn't it useful to confront them with the truth?

This nonconsequentialist view does require public school teachers to walk a tight line with respect to their treatment of controversial views and diverse life styles, but there is a line to be walked.

We may return to J. S. Mill for a consequentialist view of diversity. Mill argued for what he calls individuality by claiming that tolerating diversity has the consequence of promoting experiments in living. Just as free and open debate is necessary for seeking the truth, experiential evidence is necessary if we are to decide what are the best ways to live. Mill thus argues for individuality as a way to conduct experiments in living. We can only learn from one another about good ways to live if diversity and experimentation are valued and protected.

Mill presents other arguments for diversity. For example, he argues that diversity in ways of life makes life more varied and interesting. Diversity adds to the intrinsic interest of societies. Mill also claims that different people find their happiness in different ways. We have different tastes and needs. A society without diversity would require everyone to find their happiness in the same things. However, significant diversity allows people to find a way of living that fits their own conception of happiness.

Thus, in a variety of ways, Mill argues that diversity contributes to the greatest good for the greatest number.

Mill wants to distinguish between areas of life over which government or society may assume control and those over which individuals are sovereign. Mill draws the distinction between the public sphere and the private sphere differently than nonconsequentialists. As a consequentialist, his views emphasize the consequences of actions or ideas more than respecting personal choice. However, for most practical purposes Mill and the majority of nonconsequentialists would agree about which things should be regarded as appropriately under public control and which should be seen as private. Concerning our cases, both Mill and nonconsequentialists would view speech, religion, culture, and life style—people's conceptions of a good life—as their own business. However, they would do so in a way that rejects relativism. Inquiry into the truth about ideas and about ways of life is an important goal for Mill and for nonconsequentialists as well. Such inquiry requires intellectual liberty and experiments in living, open debate and experiential evidence, dialogue. Mill would regard two different attitudes toward truth as destructive of dialogue. The first is certainty: If we are sure we have the truth, why dialogue? The other is skepticism: If there is no truth to be found, why dialogue? Mill encourages an attitude of fallibilism—the view that inquiry into the truth has a point, but that we can never be certain that we have the truth.

## PROS AND CONS

We have now stated three different justifications for tolerating diversity. Consider some pros and cons about them. First some objections to the standard nonconsequentialist and consequentialist analyses.

1. We think that the view on respect for persons does not adequately reflect the extent to which the self is socially formed. Few of us think of ourselves as just abstract "persons." We are rather "situated selves" formed by our histories, cultures, religions, and much else besides. Moreover, this idea does not adequately reflect how we think about valuing people. Few of us wish to be valued merely because we are persons. (Of course, few of us wish to be valued merely because of our group identity either.) We want to be valued because of the particular people we as individuals happen to be. How affirmed are we likely to feel when we are informed by someone that our rights are respected because we are persons, but of course our religion is false, our culture worthless, and our achievements insignificant? Heaven save us from such praise! A view that detaches the value of persons from their "situated selves" and attaches it only to abstract personhood has missed

something. We may all be persons, but we are all also particular people who need to be valued for that reason. Our particularity as well as our personhood needs to be considered in an adequate ethic.

2.  While we do not think that the form of cultural relativism we have described above is defensible, we do think that something we shall call "modest relativism" is true. Modest relativism seeks to acknowledge two things. First, any adequate view of rationality has to acknowledge that the concepts that people acquire from their culture and their education influence and structure their perception of the world. Second, what people take to be true is often colored not just by what it is reasonable to believe, but by their interests and biases. Sometimes reasoning can be nothing more than a way of pretending that our particular interests and biases are somehow rooted in the nature of things instead of our own interests.

Hillary Putnam describes the idea that thought always occurs within the context of shared concepts: "There are two points that must be balanced, both points that been made by philosophers of many different kinds: (1) talk about what is 'right' and 'wrong' in any area only makes sense against the background of an inherited tradition; but (2) traditions themselves can be criticized."[10]

The way Putnam puts the point is designed to show that all reasoning occurs within a tradition. However, it is not intended to show that criticism and debate between traditions is impossible or that what we take to be rationality is nothing more than an expression of our interests and biases. Indeed, we think that to accept Putnam's point is to see that dialogue and argument between different traditions, religions, or cultures is essential if we are to discover our blind spots and have our biases brought to light. It is the only way that we can learn to see in another way.

There is another side to our "moderate relativism." Mill's "experiments in living" argument does not assume that all differences in how people choose to live are just experiments in which eventually when we get enough evidence we will learn what the best way to live really is. Mill also believes that people find their happiness in different ways. If this is true, then a society that permits people to pursue their happiness as they experience it will be the more conducive to the greatest happiness.

There is much to be said for this view, but it does not express a clear sense of the extent to which what people experience as valuable in their lives is a function of their culture. If, like our concepts, our happiness is socially formed, then perhaps it is at least equally important for us to value

---

10.  Hillary Putnam, *Realism and Reason* (Cambridge, England: Cambridge University Press, 1983), p. 234.

pluralism as it is to value individuality. To value pluralism is to value more than just diversity. It is to recognize that religion, culture—the things that not only make us diverse but which divide us into groups—provide the resources that make diversity and choice possible. They form both our ways of valuing and the objects of our values. Pluralism is a precondition of diversity. We need a more "groupish" vision of diversity than Mill's conception of individualism provides.

Moreover, a recognition of cultural variation in standards of value may help us to avoid biased cultural critique. Experiments are judged success-ful or not according to some standards. How are we to judge Mill's experi-ments in living? What standards of success shall we use? Are we to use the standards of the Englishmen of the nineteenth century? Mill's country and his century were notorious in judging other people's "experiments in liv-ing" as failures when compared with their own. Moreover, when they judged others to be savages, they found justification for imperialism and domination. Mill himself gives way to such sentiments in On Liberty, where he argues that paternalism is appropriate both for children and sav-ages. Arguably, if we do not have a sense of the extent to which standards of value are socially formed and what counts as happiness is culturally de-pendent, we will end up uncritically using the standards of our culture to judge others, and we will fail to respect or to learn from their experience.

Is this not cultural relativism? No. At least not in the sense we described above. We have not denied the possibility of criticizing other cultures or of learning from them. However, recognizing the variability of cultural stan-dards of value should help us in avoiding naive or biased critique, in pre-venting us from seeing our values as absolute, and in finding a middle ground between absolutism and relativism.

Mill's view also suggests that we should not assume that there must always be a right and a wrong about differences or in how people seek their happiness. Taste in food is a useful example. People's taste in food is obviously a matter of what is valued and served in their family or in their culture. They may learn to like other kinds of food as well. Or perhaps they will not. But it remains true that tastes are not just a function of some in-nate tendency to like some things and not others. They are culturally pack-aged. Even if we learn to like the food of other cultures, the standards of taste we develop from our own will condition what we learn to like in other food, and how. Again, Mill's argument for individualism might be viewed as an argument for pluralism. We should respect the tastes of dif-ferent cultures because they constitute both the standards of value and the objects of value of these cultures in a way that is not always amenable to judgments of inferiority or superiority—truth or error. Culture is often the reason why people find their happiness in different ways.

Thus, we do believe that an adequate ethical theory needs to come to terms both with the extent to which selves are more than persons and with the "concept embeddedness" of perception, thought, and value. But we also think that the formulation of the argument for radical pluralism we described above, while it does take these things into account, has some serious flaws.

One weakness of radical pluralism is that it has difficulty explaining why we should regard people as equal and as possessed of equal rights. Cultural relativism seeks to make all people equal by making all cultures equal. It does this by denying that there are any criteria that could be discovered that could be used to appraise different cultures. But how does this make either individuals or cultures equal? Indeed, since cultures need respect only their own standards of value, what is it that requires people to suspend these standards of value when judging other cultures? Is it not at least equally plausible to judge others by the standards of one's own culture even when that leads to a negative view of other cultures? Why not?

The cultural relativist can hardly say that we must tolerate other cultures because tolerance is an objective value. Nor can the relativist claim that equality is an objective value. There are no objective values. There are only the values of particular cultures to which their members are entitled. Suppose culture A holds values that lead A's to find the culture of B's worthless and the members of B inferior. What are the grounds for asserting equality and tolerance against the views of the A's? If cultural relativism is true, there can be no such grounds that are not just the values of a particular culture, and thus there can be no grounds that the A's should accept.

Cultural relativism seems parasitic on a tradition of tolerance and equality that derives from the ethics of modernity. It insists that we value other people and other cultures as equals and claims that the ethics of modernity fails to do so. But it can provide no grounds of its own for either tolerance or equality and seems to have no argument to make to intolerant cultures.

The kind of relativism that makes all truth the truth of some group or culture undermines the very meaningfulness of appraisals of value. If standards of value are entirely relative, then every culture's standards of value are equally arbitrary. To assert that something is valuable makes a claim about that thing that goes beyond the mere fact that we happen to value it. It is to claim that this object meets standards of appraisal that have a claim on others for their consideration. Consider an example. Suppose that someone, being in a romantic mood, tells someone else that she is beautiful. Is this a real compliment if we believe that there are no standards of beauty? "Darling, there are no objective standards of beauty, and you are beautiful," lacks something as a compliment. We might believe that there are objective standards of beauty and also consistently believe that beauty comes in different forms. We might believe that it can be expressed or seen differently in different cultures. We might believe that we can come to see beauty in different ways. We might believe that had we been taught or encultured differently, we might find something to be beautiful that does not seem so to us now. In short, we might believe many things about beauty that permit beauty to have significant cultural variation. But all of these things also suggest that other ways of seeing beauty might have a claim on us. We might come to appreciate what other people see as beauty. They could explain it. We could come to understand. Not only does cultural relativism not support such views, it undermines them by making all standards of value entirely arbitrary.

What we cannot do is to say (in effect), "My beloved, there are no objective standards of beauty, and you are beautiful." Cultural relativism says nothing about a given "value" other than that a given culture holds it. But this makes no claim on us for considering this value in any of the ways suggested above. Instead of earning our respect for this value, it destroys any possibility of that respect by also claiming that nothing could be pointed to about that value that could have a claim on anyone who did not currently hold it.

Relativism also undermines criticism where it is most important. If truth is relative and every culture owns its own truth, then it is impossible to criticize the values of other cultures. Indeed, this is the intent of the position. It is designed to liberate minorities from the majority's making its standards obligatory for everyone. However, it also undermines our capacity to criticize minorities or majorities when criticism seems important or warranted. Some cultural practices we might want to criticize are slavery, economic exploitation, sexually degrading views and practices, and religious intolerance and persecution. If all truth is relative to a given culture and if cultures own their own truth, on what basis do we reject or criticize these? Indeed, radical pluralism may be used as a warrant for oppressive cultures to insist that it is their right to hold and act on their views.

Finally, radical pluralism is anti-dialogical. We would like to recommend the view that cultural conflict should be resolved through a kind of dialogue that views everyone as an equal participant and insists that the outcome should depend on the evidence, not only on power or on who is the majority. If we believe that culture significantly influences how people see the world, and that people have a right to their own culture so long as they respect the equal rights of others, we may find that we have reason to listen carefully to what others different from ourselves have to say, and we may be cautious before we assume that we know the truth or that our values are superior. We may encounter other cultures with a willingness both to criticize and to learn. However, if we are to engage in dialogue of this sort, we will also have to believe that it has a point. We will have to believe that we can give others reasons to change their minds and that they can give us reasons that may change our minds.

Cultural relativism, however, denies that there are any reasons that have validity between cultures. What then is the point of dialogue?

What kind of view do we need? We need a view that acknowledges the importance of our "situatedness" to our sense of self—one in which we are not merely persons—and also acknowledges that our sense of the good is significantly dependent on our culture. But this view must do this while at the same time (1) providing some reason for belief in equality and tolerance that can be viewed as objective, (2) not undermining the very possibility of value, (3) not undermining the possibility of criticizing injustice, and (4) not undercutting the meaningfulness of dialogue.

## PERSONS AS CITIZENS

In the next chapter, we will discuss a view of ethical reasoning that emphasizes a process of formulating and testing principles that seem to capture our moral intuitions. There we will suggest that this process is consistent with a view that our moral intuitions are significantly the product of socialization or culture. Here we want to reconsider the idea of personhood in a way that makes it central to an ethic that emphasizes freedom and equality, but allows us to recognize that people are situated and have selves that are more than just persons.[11]

In this book we have tried to describe what it means to be a person in terms of the human capacities that describe personhood. We have not taken ourselves to be describing some "metaphysical" essence of people that is independent of what we can observe about them. Instead, in characterizing persons, we are describing capacities that all normal human beings acquire, given adequate nurturance. People have a capacity for a sense of justice, and they have a capacity for forming a conception of their own good.

While it is clear that views of justice and of the good are rooted in culture, it is central to our concept of a person that people have the capacity both to view their understandings of justice and the good as objects of criticism and to change their minds for reasons. Whatever a self is, it is not situated in culture in a way that prevents achieving the distance required

---

11. These views are significantly indebted to John Rawls, *Political Liberalism* (New York: Columbia University Press, 1993). Again we have developed our own account of these views and have not tried to be faithful to the details of his.

for reflection and criticism. This capacity for critical distance is an important part of what we mean by calling people responsible moral agents.

It is true that there are cultural influences on the shape the capacities that characterize persons take. However, to hold that the very idea that there are such capacities is itself based in the experience of some particular group—white European men, for example—is to hold that other groups are incapable of a view of justice or a conception of their own good, or, even worse, that they are incapable of reflecting on the moral content they receive from their culture.

The ethical concepts we have discussed in the previous chapters—due process, intellectual liberty, equality—are all concepts that have legal standing in our society and in all liberal democracies. We do not view these concepts as the whole of ethics so much as a civic ethic, and we have emphasized a civic ethic in this book because we are writing a book on ethics for people who will work in public schools where the civic ethic must be central.

Similarly, we think that our view of a person is the view of human beings that needs to be emphasized in a civic ethic. Indeed, it is precisely the conception of human beings that is important to the civic ethic of a pluralistic society Why?

The reason is that in many civic contexts we need a concept of persons that abstracts from differences. The reason isn't that people aren't different or that these differences aren't important in civic contexts. It is that the civic ethic needs to be constructed in such a way that it is not biased against people because of their group memberships or their particularities. It needs to be impartial between the conflicting interests, views, and values of different religions, races, ethnic groups, and genders.

Impartiality doesn't mean that the distinctive features of people can't be considered in public contexts. It means that the basic rules and standards society functions by can't be devised to inherently benefit one group over another. We can't prefer Catholics to Protestants, Jews, or Muslims. We can't prefer men to women. We can't prefer white people to African Americans, Native Americans, or Asian Americans.

Think of what is required on the analogy of a sporting event. Impartiality doesn't require that we ignore who is stronger, faster, or more skilled. It requires that the rules not be rigged in ways that are irrelevant to the point of the game. Similarly, we need a view of social justice that gives people a fair chance to pursue their own conception of their own good without rigging the game to prefer the interests of some over others.

A concept of human beings as free and equal persons who are therefore entitled to equal liberty and equal treatment helps us to conceive and sustain a society that respects pluralism. It does so by focusing attention on the status that people have as citizens and making that central to a concept of social justice. And it does this by abstracting from the features of people that make them different in order to ground the basic rules of our society in a way that is fair and unbiased in that it does not assume that any one group is privileged in society.

Does this concept of a person describe some essence of people they have prior to being socialized? No. Indeed, development of the capacities involved in personhood requires socialization. Does it deny that people are situated or the ethical relevance of their situatedness? No. Their situatedness is an important aspect of who real people are that needs to be taken into account in dealing with them. Is it a view that subtly makes the characteristics of some particular group, white males perhaps, normative for everyone? We don't think so. One needs to be careful of the details, however, and open criticism and dialogue are important to the process of taking care that this isn't so.

Thus, properly formulated, the notion of personhood and the civic ethic toward which it points are defensible. Indeed, they seem to us to be crucial for a defensible pluralism. But we need to recognize that people are social beings, that they are not just persons but situated particular beings, and that religion, culture, ethnicity, and gender are important to that particular person who each of us is. These facts are especially important to take into account in a view of moral dialogue, because they remind us that we need to be sensitive to different voices and to be careful to not universalize our own particularities.

## AN ADDITIONAL CASE

Before going on to the next chapter, you may want to consider an additional case about multicultural and religious differences. The major Christian holiday of Christmas is celebrated in this and many other countries where there are minorities who are not Christian. Is this being sensitive to a civic ethic of different voices? Is this universalizing one group's particularities?

### A Christmas Quarrel

Tenderville is a well established, middle-class community. Its roots go back to the early 1800s, but it didn't become a full-fledged township until 1936. World War II gave it a growth spurt, and it boomed in the 1950s. Its citizens were proud of its excellent school system, good library, and extensive community services. In the 1960s and 1970s it attracted many white collar workers from the nearby big city as a tranquil haven and good place to raise children. It was one of the first northern towns to voluntarily and successfully desegregate its schools. Everyone seemed to get along very well together. Because of its openness and friendliness, a Jewish community moved in, establishing its own synagogue. In the 1980s and 1990s many Asians also were attracted to Tenderville. It seemed to be a haven of tolerance and real democracy.

Then it happened.

The acute sensitivity to the worth of others and the great and genuine tolerance of difference that permeated the town stimulated a seriously responsible school board to raise the issue of Christmas in the schools. Christmas had always been celebrated with Nativity plays, Christmas caroling, decorated trees, exchanges of presents, and of course, the Christmas vacation. But the Board began to wonder out loud about how this civic celebration of a major Christian event would feel to those who were Jews, Muslims, Buddhists, Confucianists, or atheists. There seemed to be something askew here. Just as Tenderville had grown from a small Christian community to a larger multicultural and multireligious community, should not the school system do the same? But how?

There were a number of suggestions made at the Board meeting. Here are some of them and some of the objections to them voiced at the public meeting.

The superintendent suggested that for starters, he would issue a policy that the schools should not have any decorations, songs, activities, or talk, written or oral, about Christmas. The holiday vacation name would be officially changed to Winter Recess. No gift giving in school would be allowed. All trappings of Christmas then would just disappear, thereby solving the problem. The superintendent said that he and his principals would strictly enforce this no-Christmas policy, if the Board agreed to his plan.

Some felt, however, that this would be impossible to do. It is hard to ban Christmas, given the attention it gets in the environment outside of school. Besides, the kids are full of it. Maybe it would be better to recognize and teach about Christmas and also about Chanukah as major religious holidays of winter. After all, the combined population of Christians and Jews in Tenderville was over 85%. But, some wondered, what about the mix of other religions in the remaining 15%? Should they not also get their due, and have one of their major religious holidays celebrated in school?

Someone quickly raised the question of separation of church and state. Isn't the school constitutionally obliged to stay away from religious teaching, either directly or indirectly? "But," someone in the back of the auditorium called out, "doesn't being tolerant require understanding another's point of view? How is that possible if you don't learn about what others believe?"

The meeting went on well past midnight. The remarkable thing was that there was no venom, no "we" against "them," no unalterable oppositions. It was a genuine attempt to find a sensible and sound way to continue the good feeling of a community of inclusion, but the solution always seemed just out of reach.

*Some Questions*

1. If you had attended this meeting what suggestions would you have made?
2. Does the separation of church and state doctrine disallow any talk or teaching about religion in the public schools? What does it allow?
3. Does practicing tolerance require understanding the basis of differences, or just respecting difference even if you don't understand the grounds for it?
4. There are multicultural as well as multireligious differences in the school population of Tenderville. Should different cultures also be addressed in school policy and the school's curriculum? How?

## FOR FURTHER INQUIRY

Appiah, Kwame Anthony. *The Ethics of Identity.* Princeton, NJ: Princeton University Press, 2005.
> A discussion of the role of personal identity in ethics.

Banks, James A. *Multicultural Education, Transformative Knowledge, and Action.* New York: Teachers College Press, 1996.
> A discussion of multiculturalism from the foremost educational scholar on the topic.

Bull, Barry L.; Fruehling, Royal T.; and Chattergy, Virgie. *The Ethics of Multicultural and Bilingual Education.* New York: Teachers College Press, 1992.
> A discussion of multiculturalism and bilingualism that compares a liberal, a democratic, and a communitarian approach.

Galston, Robert. "Church, State and Education." In *A Companion to the Philosophy of Education,* edited by Randall Curren, 412–29. Oxford: Blackwell, 2003.
> A discussion of religious liberty in education.

Feinberg, Walter. *Common Schools: Uncommon Identities.* New Haven, CT: Yale University Press, 1998.
> A discussion of how to balance pluralism and the need for a shared American identity.

Fullinwider, Robert. "Multicultural Education." In *A Companion to the Philosophy of Education,* edited by Randall Curren, 487–500. Oxford: Blackwell, 2003.
> A discussion of multiculturalism.

Macedo, Stephen. *Diversity and Distrust.* Cambridge, MA: Harvard University Press, 2000.
    This book discusses the nature of citizenship in a society characterized by durable pluralism.

Mill, John Stuart. *On Liberty.* Indianapolis, IN: Bobbs-Merrill, 1956.
    The classic arguments for freedom of opinion and lifestyle. The arguments of Chapter 3 emphasize what Mill calls "Individuality."

Rawls, John. *Political Liberalism.* New York: Columbia University Press, 1993.
    Rawls rethinks the argument of *A Theory of Justice.* He argues that justice as fairness must be viewed as a political theory, but not a comprehensive moral doctrine. Justice must be an overlapping consensus of political ideals shared by diverse comprehensive doctrines.

Strike, Kenneth A. "Is Liberal Education Illiberal? Political Liberalism and Liberal Education." In *Philosophy of Education,* 2004, 121–29. Urbana, Illinois: Philosophy of Education Society, 2005.
    A discussion of teaching with integrity that includes comments of teaching creation science and intelligent design.

Taylor, Charles. "The Politics of Recognition." In *Multiculturalism: Examining the Politics of Recognition,* edited by Amy Gutmann. Princeton, NJ: Princeton University Press, 1994.
    Taylor's essay argues that we cannot value persons unless we value the culture that formed them. He makes a prima facie case that every culture contains something of value. The companion articles in this collection, which focus on Taylor's essay, are also well worth reading.

Young, Iris Marion. *Justice and the Politics of Difference.* Princeton, NJ: Princeton University Press, 1990.
    Young criticizes the view that oppression and domination are not issues of distributive justice. Her discussion of these concepts supports a politics of difference.

*Chapter 6*

# Democracy, Professionalism, and Teaching with Integrity

## A CASE TO CONSIDER

Percy Wright, a reporter for the *New World Chronicle,* was investigating a story that had recently broken at New World West Elementary School. The case dealt with Irene Canebrake, a second grade teacher. New World was contemplating taking disciplinary action against Canebrake for refusing to comply with the district's recently approved curriculum guide for mathematics in the elementary schools. The new guide required the introduction of fractions in the second grade. It also specified a testing program for determining the mastery of various mathematical skills, including fractions. Ms. Canebrake, after attempting to teach the required curriculum, had stopped doing so. In her own defense she wrote a note to Angela Dormer, the principal of West Elementary. Her note said that, in her professional judgment, the majority of students in the second grade were not able to deal with fractions. Moreover, the frustration that resulted from being required to master material that was beyond their ability had begun to affect their work in other areas. Her classroom was no longer a happy place. Therefore, she had decided not to teach the curriculum as specified.

Angela Dormer had initially responded by having an informal talk with Ms. Canebrake in which her main message was that Canebrake was free to teach the required curriculum in any way that she saw fit, but that she was not free to ignore it. Ms. Dormer also hinted that blatant insubordination could not be ignored. Canebrake thanked Dormer for her advice, but said that it was a matter of principle with her. The curriculum was harmful to the emotional welfare and educational progress of the children in her charge. Thus she would not teach it. Nor would she engage in the hypocrisy required to pretend to do so in order to satisfy some bureaucratic requirement. If the district felt that it had to take action against her, she was willing to defend her decision before the board. She believed that her duty to her children required this.

Percy Wright had discovered the Canebrake–Dormer conflict because several parents in Irene Canebrake's class had gotten involved. They believed that publicity would be favorable to Canebrake, who had a reputation as an excellent teacher. They had called Wright with their story about how the "mindless bureaucrats" in the district were persecuting the best teacher in the school. Percy decided that the case might be of public interest. He interviewed both Irene Canebrake and Angela Dormer and then condensed their remarks. The following is his rendition of their positions. He thought it might make a good article if it was framed as a debate between two personal points of view. His readers would have to decide who was right.

*Irene Canebrake:* I know that Angela is just trying to do her job, but she has to be able to see this from my point of view. I am responsible for the education and the emotional welfare of these children. I am an experienced teacher. I am well trained in my field. All of my professional knowledge and experience say that this curriculum cannot be taught to these children at this age. I would be irresponsible if I tried to teach it. The children can't learn the material. Trying to teach it to them will generate negative attitudes toward mathematics and will produce unnecessary stress in my classroom. I know some people in the district worked hard on this curriculum guide, but I cannot allow myself to be required to teach in a way that is so obviously harmful to the children in my class. They are my first responsibility. To comply with this curriculum guide when I know that it is harmful to my students would be unethical. Angela should ask herself what she would do in my place. Would she be willing to mistreat these kids because of some silly piece of paper?

*Angela Dormer:* I understand that Irene is trying to do the best job that she can for her students and that she is conscientiously opposed to the curriculum guide on this matter. However, the curriculum guide was created by a district committee of parents, teachers, and administrators. There was even a sixth-grader there to represent students. They discussed the curriculum for months. They considered the question of whether second grade was too soon for fractions, and, although opinion was divided, they agreed that, in light of the need for higher standards in education, fractions should be introduced early. Even those members of the committee who continued to harbor doubts about the new curriculum eventually were persuaded to lend the policy their provisional support. Whether they are right or wrong, the point is that this curriculum guide has been worked on for a long time by a district committee, and it has been adopted by the school board.

Neither Irene nor I are free to substitute our judgment for that of the board of education. Irene should put herself in my place. Am I supposed to overlook the collective judgment of the district curriculum committee and the vote of the school board because Irene believes that they are wrong? Perhaps they are wrong. Nevertheless, I have a duty to enforce district policy.

Having digested the product of his efforts, reporter Wright has decided not to print the story. As he put it to his editor, "If Dormer had been shaking Canebrake down for a few kickbacks or if Canebrake had been molesting her students, our readers might be interested. I could see a good series on ethics in the schools resulting from that. But all these principled disagreements are tedious. I can't see our readers being interested in all this high-mindedness about whether fractions should be taught to second-graders."

Unlike the readers of the *New World Chronicle*, we have the opportunity to consider this case. Once again, the parties disagree in a way that seems unresolvable. How might we respond? Several responses seem possible. On the one hand, one might treat the disagreement as a reason for moral skepticism. The authors of this book, the reader might say, keep on insisting that ethical reasoning has a point and that it is capable of producing results, but they keep on giving us cases that they seem unable to resolve. Why should we believe that ethical reasoning can work? Don't the authors owe us a fuller account of how ethical reasoning should work to resolve such issues? On the other hand, one might treat this case as demonstrating the need for an inquiry into legitimate authority. When two parties in a dispute disagree and when some decision must be made, how do we decide who is entitled to decide? Who has the right to make the final decision? Finally, the case raises questions about the nature of the ethical deliberative process itself. One might argue that what this case calls for is more dialogue between the contesting parties. They need to talk the matter out more and come to some consensus. Maybe they stopped talking too soon. Maybe an understanding of the conditions of productive ethical dialogue needs to be spelled out.

In what follows, we will address four concerns. First, we will characterize what we call *reflective equilibrium*. This will provide a fuller description of ethical reasoning. Second, we will discuss the problem of sovereignty or authority. In schools, when people disagree, who is entitled to make the decision? Third, we will consider the ideas of teacher professionalism and teaching with integrity. Finally, we want to discuss ethical deliberation as a social process. Here we want to insist that a social process of ethical dialogue is not just nice, but necessary. Moral deliberation is inherently a social process and, as such, has some special features that are important to validating ethical decisions. We turn first to a fuller description of our view of ethical reasoning.

## REFLECTIVE EQUILIBRIUM

The reader should not be overly distressed by the many instances of moral ambiguity we have presented in this book. Ethical matters are not always so contestable. Nevertheless, the fact is that people disagree. Even when they disagree deeply and for a very long time, however, it does not mean that reasoned agreement in ethics is forever impossible. In the sciences, for example, matters that were topics of disagreement for a long time seem to get resolved eventually. Thus the existence of persistent disagreement may be taken as a reason for believing that even though a matter is difficult, it need not be unresolvable. Even in ethics, some issues about which people have long disagreed have eventually come to be resolved. For example, human beings were unclear about the morality of slavery for centuries. Yet today the immorality of slavery can be taken as an established moral principle. We also need to be careful to avoid inappropriate expectations of ethical reasoning. Ethics is more like law than math or science in its degree of precision and its aspirations. While ethics, like law, can be studied and used to deal with real problems, it is not capable of the same degree of conclusiveness as mathematics; and its purpose is not to achieve a description of the world as it is, but of how it ought to be. We see the purpose of ethical deliberation as seeking to achieve agreement on principles that regulate human action while respecting the equal worth and the interests of all. We suggest that reflective equilibrium is the appropriate standard for such an activity and that extensive dialogue is a requirement for its achievement.

We will begin our account of reflective equilibrium with a brief sketch of our position. The central ideas are these: Moral decisions regarding choice and action require moral sensitivity, rationality, and the development of moral theory for which the primary evidence is our moral intuitions. Moral intuitions, our sense of what is right and wrong, are the basic data for moral reasoning and the construction of moral theory.

Not every moral intuition is equally useful, however. We should begin with those which seem compelling and uncontroversial. Constructing a moral theory then proceeds through attempts to formulate principles that account for these moral intuitions. We must be able to describe the underlying moral concepts that generate our sense of right and wrong, to discover the implicit rules that cause us to feel the way we do. It is not just taking whatever pops into our hearts and heads as right or wrong; it is looking for the bases of our intuitions, describing and analyzing them, and then testing them to the best of our ability.

In this respect, constructing a moral theory is much like attempting to describe the rules governing our sense of grammar. We have intuitions about how to use language correctly and meaningfully without necessarily being able to formulate the rules of our language. This sense of what is meaningful or correct to say provides the data against which to test sets of rules postulated in order to explain our sense of grammar. In fact, that is how grammarians do grammar. They will ask themselves questions such as "Why does 'All good boys eat cake' make sense and 'Cake boys good eat all' not make sense?" Likewise, we must make clear and explicit the rules and principles that underlie our moral intuitions.

The analogy goes even deeper. Sometimes a deep understanding of the principles of language can lead us to revise our initial opinion about what is meaningful or correct. Understanding the principle can make an expression that seemed obscure or ambiguous clear and comprehensible, or it can lead us to see the awkwardness or obscurity of something that had appeared clear and simple. Likewise, a moral theory can change or overrule our intuitions about moral phenomena. Once we see more clearly what is assumed by our moral intuitions, we may wish to change them. Thus, there is an interaction between moral theory and moral intuition in ethical reflection, each influencing the other. The trick is to achieve some point of reflective equilibrium between our moral sense and our moral theory. By reflective equilibrium we mean reaching a point in our deliberations where we feel that our moral intuitions and the moral theory that accounts for them are satisfactorily consistent and where the decisions we reach and actions we take can be justified by our moral theory. Of course, as with scientific theory, new facts, events, and hypotheses can force us to reconsider and reformulate our moral theory and to alter our decisions and actions.

Moral theories must meet the standards common to judging theories of all sorts. They must explain the data appropriate to them. They must be consistent. Elegance, parsimony, and symmetry are nice, too, when they can be had. Moral theories must also be sensitive to knowledge in other domains. Factual matters and the theories of other disciplines are important to ethical theory, not only because they are important in knowing how moral abstractions are applied to concrete cases, but also because they can suggest new problems to be solved or alter the concepts by means of which ethical theories are articulated. Freud's discovery of the unconscious raised difficult questions for the notion of autonomy and posed new moral issues about psychological manipulation. The advances of physics and biology drove purposes from nature and required people to rethink the way in which values and purposes exist. These are things that any comprehensive moral theory must confront.

Having a comprehensive and well thought out moral theory is not enough. As feeling human beings we also need to be sensitive to the moral domain and draw upon our shared ability to empathize with and care about other persons. Our moral intuitions are rooted in our ability to feel and empathize as well as in our ability to think. We need both emotion and reason to be moved to act morally as well as to care about rational moral arguments and their outcomes. Feelings interact with moral reasoning in several important ways. First, feelings help us to put ourselves in the place of others, to identify with them, to know what hurts and what helps. It will do little good to be committed to respecting the value and dignity of other persons if we cannot experience life from their point of view. How else shall we know how to respect them? How else shall we discover what counts as affirming their dignity?

Second, feelings provide motivation for right conduct. If one could build a computer capable of engaging in moral reasoning, its chief defect would probably be that it would not care about being moral. Knowing what is right and wanting to do it are different things. Our ability to empathize, to experience the wrong done to others as our hurt and the good done to others as our joy, is a large part of our desire to do right. Immanuel Kant, who had many wise things to say about ethics, said nothing wiser than that the only really good thing is a good will.

How, then, do we settle ethical arguments? We proceed first by trying to discover the moral principles that underlie our differing senses of right and wrong. When we see what it is that our moral intuitions assume, perhaps some will change their minds. If not, then we must test our conflicting moral principles by seeing what else follows from them. If we find that some proposed principle leads to an abhorrent result in certain cases, that is a reason to abandon it. Perhaps some will change their minds when they see what else they must agree to if they are to hold consistently to their current principles.

We must now ask, where do our ethical intuitions come from? This question would seem to bear on how far it is possible to establish any reflective equilibrium about ethical issues that is objective. Some philosophers have argued that our sense of morality is innate. Others have suggested that moral intuitions are a kind of seeing. There are moral facts that we can see with our mind's eye, just as we see colors with our physical eye. Others assume that we learn our moral principles, just as we learn our native language, from our culture. Does it matter? One might argue that if moral concepts are innate or involve seeing moral facts that have objective existence, then that certifies the objectivity of moral thought. Moral questions, like questions about the physical world, have answers. On the other hand, if we acquire those principles that generate our moral intuitions from our culture, that means that, fundamentally, relativism is still true. The best that moral reasoning could be expected to do in that case would be to produce a higher level of agreement among those who already agree about basic assumptions.

We believe, however, that the question of where our moral intuitions come from is not that decisive. Seeing it as decisive rests on inflated demands for what will be permitted to count as objective knowledge and an excessive pessimism about human commonalities. If we demand certainty of moral knowledge or if we demand that all legitimate knowledge somehow inheres in the ultimate nature of existence, we may find knowledge difficult to come by—and not only about ethics. If we insist only on establishing a provisional reflective equilibrium, we will have set a standard for objectivity that can often be met and will serve us well in our lives. What is the point of setting our standards for objective knowledge in a way that makes a fundamental and necessary human activity, that of reflecting on what we ought to do, appear impossible?

Moreover, even if our ethical intuitions are acquired from our society, it does not follow that reflective equilibrium between members of different societies is impossible. To the degree that societies are different, we may expect the search for reflective moral equilibrium to be difficult. To assume that it is impossible is to neglect the extent to which all societies are composed of people with a common biology, common fundamental needs, a common physical environment, and common aspirations. It is also to neglect the extent to which we live on a planet whose people are increasingly united by a common science and by common global problems. These commonalities are basic to our view of the source of the moral intuitions of human beings. We are not all so alike that reflective equilibrium about moral matters is likely to be easy. We are not all so different that it must be impossible. Some of us would even argue that we see in human history writ large a positive development of a more humane and more broadly shared ethical point of view. There are, then, some good reasons to keep open the possibility of humanly arrived at ethical knowledge. We can be rational and objective without being certain, and we can be tolerant and open to other points of view without being relativists.

Nevertheless, there is a common but misguided incentive for the prevalent modern belief in moral relativism. It is the human desire to be free, to be unencumbered by duties and obligations. If we may misparaphrase Dostoevski, people seem to believe that if relativism is true, then everything is permitted. Each of us may do as we choose, and no one can tell us that we are wrong or that we must do something else. The idea is often captured in the suggestion that people who argue that something is genuinely right or wrong are in reality attempting to impose their views on others.

This response is both confused and problematic. It is confused in that it identifies compulsion with persuasion. When one person attempts to give reasons to another person, that act is not an attempt at coercion. Indeed, persuasion is a form of influence that recognizes individuals as free moral agents with rational minds and human feelings. To attempt to persuade someone is to assume that the choice is theirs and that as responsible moral agents they would wish to make it on the basis of the best reasons available. To give people reasons is to confirm their status as free people who have the right to choose for themselves.

Seeing persuasion as a kind of coercion ultimately rests on a failure to understand the ultimate moral basis of freedom. We are not free because we have no objective duties. Nothing about freedom follows from moral relativism, because nothing at all concerning ethical matters can follow from relativism. We are free because we are moral agents with the duty to decide for ourselves and because it is morally offensive to interfere arbitrarily with the liberty of a person who has the moral duty to make responsible choices.

It is often claimed that what sets human beings off from other living creatures is their ability to reason. From our point of view, we humans also share the distinctive capacity to have and choose to have obligations. To ask what moral obligations we should accept is to presume that we are free to choose and that good reasons can be given for some choices and against others. And the giving of reasons presumes that reasons provide objective grounds for reaching potential agreements and progressive states of reflective equilibrium and moral growth.

Relativism is problematic in that, if taken seriously, it can lead us to withhold resources that are important for moral growth. People do not learn to make responsible choices by being told that it does not matter what they decide, since one choice is as good as another. They learn to make responsible choices by learning to appraise arguments and consider evidence relevant to what they have to decide. Such things are best learned by participating in a milieu in which ethical matters are seriously considered and debated. Moral relativism undermines the moral education appropriate to a free people.

## THE QUESTION OF SOVEREIGNTY

Perhaps, then, in the long run, after much debate and deliberation, ethical agreement is possible. However, sometimes decisions need to be made in the short run even though people continue to disagree. Then we need to know what legitimates a decision under conditions of disagreement. What confers sovereignty (that is, the authority or right to decide)?

Consider a simple-minded position. Let us suppose that what gives a person the right to decide some matter is that the person knows what the best thing to do is. This might be the position of Irene Canebrake. She feels entitled to refuse to teach the new math curriculum simply because she *knows* that it is not in the children's best interest. However, this is not a tenable position, since in cases of conflict it is, by definition, unclear who is right. Thus it is unhelpful to claim that the person who should decide is the person who is right. We need to keep separate the question of what the right decision is from the question of what constitutes legitimacy in decision making. Both are important, of course, but we must be able to decide whether a decision is legitimate even when (especially when!) we disagree about which decision is best. How can we do this?

One response is that legitimate decisions are those achieved by a legitimate process. We might, for example, hold that decisions are legitimated by voting and that a particular decision is confirmed when it achieves a majority of votes. Such a view tells us how decisions are legitimated, and it locates sovereignty in the majority, but nothing guarantees that the decisions of a majority are the best ones.

Fortunately, there are other candidates for legitimating procedures that also speak to the question of making the right decision. Let us return to Irene Canebrake's view and see if we can describe it in a less simple-minded fashion. We might claim that the right to make decisions should be given to those who are in the best position to know what is right. On this interpretation, Irene would be claiming sovereignty over the decision, not because she is right, but because she is in the best position of all concerned parties to know what decision is best for her children. She is the trained and experienced teacher, and she best knows the children in her class. Thus she should be given the right to decide. We shall call this position, in which legitimacy is conferred by reason of expertise, *professionalism*.

Professionalism maintains that authority should be vested in those who are most capable of making the best decision. Of course, in our day, advocates of professional decision making also recognize the legitimacy of democratic processes. However, they often wish to argue that, even in a democratic society, some decisions (for example, how to conduct brain surgery) should be made not by majority vote, but by those who have special competence. Thus arguments for professionalism are arguments about when democratic authority is inappropriate or ineffective and when the power to decide is best vested in an expert individual or professional group.

One purpose of democratic decision making is to make sure that everyone's interest in a decision is fairly considered. However, when individuals or special groups gain unencumbered power to make decisions about public matters, they may make these decisions in ways that are most attentive to their own welfare. As Lord Acton noted, power tends to corrupt. Democracy addresses this problem by giving everyone equal power over public decisions and a voice in public deliberations. In representative democracies these things are accomplished (imperfectly) by elections and by such rights as free speech and a free press and freedom of petition and assembly. Elected officials represent the people and must undergo scrutiny and criticism. When the people disapprove of how they are represented, they may vote the rascals out.

Nevertheless, there may be cases in which democracy is especially ineffective in protecting the public interest. Some decisions may require "esoteric knowledge." Esoteric knowledge is knowledge that is not available to the ordinary person, usually because it is the product of lengthy training. When decisions require esoteric knowledge to be made competently, democratic institutions may be ineffective means for making these decisions because the citizenry or their elected representatives may lack the competence to evaluate the decisions adequately. In such cases, it may be desirable to vest those who possess the required knowledge, the experts, with authority.

Often professional authority is exercised by a professional organization that is explicitly empowered to make certain decisions by a democratic body such as a state legislature. Such organizations are given three interconnected powers. First, they are given the authority to legitimate a knowledge base. They engage in a variety of deliberative processes that result in the identification of what is to count as professional knowledge and how it is to be assessed. Second, they govern the professional practice of their members. They do this by prescribing what counts as competent practice and by disciplining members who practice incompetently or unethically. Finally, professions control the initiation of new members into the profession. They do this both by prescribing and conducting their education and by determining the qualifications for licensure.

When authority over decisions is transferred to professionals, how are we to be sure that it is exercised in the interest of the people? The usual response to this question is that professionals are taught an ethic that emphasizes maintaining professional standards and client welfare. Thus it is the training of professionals, their initiation into an ethic of professional responsibility and service, that primarily serves to ensure that professionals serve the public.

Irene Canebrake's argument makes the most sense if one sees it as an expression of professionalism in education. She has appealed to her training and experience, her expertise, to legitimate her authority over the math curriculum in her class. She has claimed that she should make the decision because she is in a position to make the best decision. She has also made a strong appeal to an ethic of professionalism. She has claimed that her first duties are to her profession and its standards of good practice and to the welfare of the children in her classroom. These duties outweigh her responsibilities to her administrative superiors and to the school board.

Does this argument succeed? In one respect it is clear that it does not. It is currently the case that the law locates sovereignty over education not in teachers or their organizations, but in state legislatures and in school boards, both of which are elected legislative bodies. Such bodies may choose to respect the decisions of the teachers they employ, but they are not obliged to do so. Legally, teaching is not currently structured as a profession.

Perhaps this is unwise. The public interest in education might be better served if teaching was recognized as a profession and if teachers had more autonomy in their work. This is an issue that is currently being hotly debated. Moreover, it is a complex issue that cannot be decided here. But we do wish to make a few observations about it.

In our society arguments in favor of professionalizing teaching are often arguments against the democratic governance of education. If teachers are to govern their own practice, then the right of state legislatures or local school boards to make an extensive range of educational decisions will have to be diminished or restricted. A new division of labor between elected authorities and professional teachers will have to be forged. Sovereignty over education will be relocated. That professionalism is competitive with democracy in this way does not mean that it is undesirable or incompatible. But it does mean that a case must be made that is adequate to rebut a presumption in favor of democratic authority. This is true even when expert knowledge is required in decision making.

Such a case requires two things. First, there must be an adequate knowledge base to ground a profession of teaching. The crucial feature of Irene Canebrake's case for authority over the conduct of her classroom is that she, and not others, is in a position to know what is best for her students. If such claims are a basis for professionalism, then teachers must possess expert knowledge that is genuinely esoteric. Teachers must be like doctors in that their education renders them uniquely capable of making competent professional choices. Second, the education teachers receive must be sufficient to establish an ethic of professional responsibility and client welfare. It is such an ethic that ensures that professional autonomy serves the public interest.

Angela Dormer's case against Irene Canebrake is an argument for democratic authority. Angela regards herself as entitled to enforce the school district's curriculum policy because that policy was democratically arrived at and because she has been appointed by the duly constituted democratic authority to administer its decisions. The curriculum policy was developed by a suitably representative committee consisting of parents, teachers, and administrators. It was adopted by the school board. Angela does not argue that this process is the one that is most likely to make the best decision. Instead she seems to claim that the decision is legitimate because it was democratically achieved.

Angela regards her own authority as deriving from the authority of the board of education. She was hired by them to implement their decisions. Consequently, she is bound by board policy. She sees Irene as similarly obligated. In accepting employment by the New World School District, Irene has become a public servant bound by the authority of democratically elected officials. To assert her judgment against theirs is to reject the legitimacy of democratic authority.

If we look closely we will see that Angela's arguments appeal to two different visions of what democracy is about. Initially, Angela appeals to the fact that the curriculum policy was created by a committee that represented various interests in the school, that the committee engaged in extensive deliberations, and that eventually all members of the committee agreed. Later, however, Angela appeals to the fact that the committee's policy was adopted by the school board as her central argument. She seems to regard the school board as the final authority and sees her own authority as deriving from the board's.

The two visions of democracy expressed in these two different arguments can be distinguished from each other. In the first argument, Angela appeals to what we call *communitarian democracy*. It has three central features. First, it takes the participants in the democratic process to be those individuals who are currently within the school community. Second, it emphasizes the importance of discussion and rational deliberation in decision making. Third, it seeks consensus and tries to avoid circumstances in which majorities enforce their will on minorities.

This view of democracy seems committed to the idea that decisions are legitimated when they are the product of uncoerced discussion and consensus among community members. The community here is not the larger community of citizens who live within the boundaries of the school district. It consists of those who are, in one way or another, directly involved in the school. Moreover, it tends to see deliberation and consensus as more important than voting in legitimating decisions.

Angela emphasizes that the district's policy is legitimated because it was achieved by such a process. The appeal of the argument to Irene Canebrake is best described as an appeal to her sense of identification with the school community. Angela is saying to Irene: "Look, this is what we decided. In resisting the decision, you are withdrawing from the community. You seem no longer to be one of us." The view that affiliation is cemented by open participation and that resisting the consensus once achieved ruptures the community is a significant part of the ethos of any democratic community and a powerful means of legitimating decisions.

This view of democracy does not provide an adequate account of sovereignty in public schools. Public schools are financed by taxes, which are collected, directly or indirectly, from state and local citizens. Moreover, these citizens have interests in the quality and character of education even when they do not directly participate in the affairs of the school. Thus the curriculum committee, as constituted in this case, does not represent the interests of taxpayers or other citizens. If sovereignty over educational decisions were to reside in such internal committees and if educational decisions could be made by participants in the school in a way that was unchecked by the larger community, then several important tenets of democracy would be violated. There would be taxation without representation. Citizens of the community would find themselves unable to influence schools even though they were taxed to pay for them, were required to send their children to them, and underwent the consequences of the success or failure of the education provided. These are all reasons to hold that sovereignty must reside outside the immediate school community and should be vested in the elected representatives of the citizenry. Let us call this form of democracy *representative democracy.*

An appeal to representative democracy is Angela Dormer's trump card in her disagreement with Irene Canebrake. In a democratic society sovereignty over public education ultimately rests in elected legislative bodies. To oppose the authority of the school board is to oppose representative democracy.

In our society, given its political traditions, it is hard not to agree that ultimately Angela Dormer is right. At the same time, we should note the dark side of representative democracy. School districts are typically large entities. Their boundaries may include thousands or even millions of citizens. They may employ hundreds or even thousands of teachers and administrators, and they may teach many thousands of students. Given such large organizations, it is unlikely that school board members will be able to participate directly in the affairs of any given school. Instead, school boards will make policy and hire administrators to implement it. Teachers will be employees who owe a duty to their employer. They may or may not exercise independent judgment as their employer decides, but to resist the will of their employer once expressed is to commit the sin of insubordination against democratic authority. Such schools are likely to be hierarchically organized. Teachers will be the lowest link in a chain of command. Locating sovereignty in a remote legislative body can make teachers into people who merely implement decisions made elsewhere, by individuals whose competence in matters of education is far from assured. This may deny teachers a voice in policy and may deny schools the benefit of their wisdom and their involvement in decision making. In some cases it may force on them a choice between their professional ethic and their duty to their employer. Even if Irene Canebrake's professionalism argument is insufficient to entitle her to sovereignty over what goes on in her classroom, we should not ignore the fact that she may indeed be the person who is in the best position to know what is best for her children.

These observations suggest two conclusions. One is that in considering how decisions are to be made in schools there are different views of how to locate authority that serve different values. Professionalism emphasizes expertise and competence, communitarian democracy emphasizes participation and discussion, and representative democracy emphasizes equal representation of the citizenry. All of these values seem commendable. At the same time, it seems difficult to serve them all simultaneously. A second conclusion is that, whenever disagreement is so deep that we must raise the issue of sovereignty, in our society we must conclude that sovereignty rests in the people unless the people vest it elsewhere. This means that teachers, who are not legally professionals, will have to respect the decisions of legislatures, even if they regard them as wrong. (Of course, this does not mean that there are no legal or morally right ways to contest bad decisions. Nor does it mean that teachers are not entitled to pursue professional status for themselves.)

## PROFESSIONALISM AND TEACHING WITH INTEGRITY

For Irene Canebrake this is not just an issue about sovereignty or how to resolve a disagreement. For Irene this is a matter of conscience. Her integrity is at stake. If the decision continues to go against her, she may be compelled to behave in ways she sees as unprofessional and harmful. More needs to be said about what teachers should do when they are expected, as a part of their jobs, to engage in activities that they think to be unwise. Tensions between teachers' best judgment and job requirements have grown in recent years because changes in educational policy have increased external control over classroom practice and have decreased the autonomy of teachers. Schools and teachers are increasingly judged by results on standardized tests that measure student mastery of content specified in state-approved curricula. Teachers are expected to teach what is to be tested, and what counts as best practice is specified for them. Other policies, such as zero tolerance laws and assertive discipline programs, specify disciplinary practices. We do not argue here that these practices are misconceived or generally harmful. Such practices do, however, erode the autonomy of teachers over their classrooms and their teaching, and they can lead to tension between teachers' integrity and what they are required to do under these policies. What does it mean to teach with integrity, and what should teachers do when their integrity is called into question?

Suppose Irene had said, "I have been teaching for a long time, and I'm good at it. My experience indicates that this practice is harmful to children. My feelings about this and my personal moral code prohibits me from doing what I believe harms kids." While we respect teachers who have convictions about their practice, we think this is a weak answer. It grounds Irene's resistance to the policies of her school in her own experience and her personal feelings about it. Compare this response to a second possibility: "I have reviewed the literature on this topic, and I have discussed it with other teachers who have tried teaching fractions to young children. There is a consensus, supported by research and experience, that trying to teach fractions to children this young routinely fails and does emotional harm. Moreover, the Society for the Teaching of Elementary Mathematics has developed a set of practice guidelines that indicates that fractions should not be taught until the later elementary grades. We know this practice is harmful. I cannot in good conscience do it."

In both of these justifications Irene has claimed that her sense of integrity is violated. In the second case, however, she affirms two important ideas. First, she claims that there is a body of knowledge that supports her view. It is not just her private opinion; it is what the research shows and what the collective experience of many teachers confirms. Second, she claims that her professional society has recognized and affirmed this body of knowledge and has expressed it in a set of guidelines. As a result, Irene has a professional warrant for her view that is rooted in the standards of her profession. This warrant has two features: There is a body of research, experience, and argument that supports her view, and her professional community has recognized this body of evidence. Evidence and peer affirmation—and not personal opinion—are the essence of a professional warrant.

In addition to claiming a professional warrant for her views, Irene has claimed that her knowledge and her community have shaped her conscience and her sense of integrity. It is not just that she has personal feelings about this matter; it is also that she has internalized the norms of her profession, and these norms shape her judgment and her conscience. Her professionalism and her sense of integrity are connected. Above, we said that the case for professionalism rested not only on the idea that professionals possess knowledge that puts them in a position to make good decisions, but also on the belief that the practice of professionals is governed by an ethic that emphasizes professional responsibility and client welfare. The second response suggests that this is the case for Irene.

Obviously we prefer the second response. Why? When Irene puts her concerns this way, she makes the matter objective and assessable, and she invokes the authority of her professional community. She has told her colleagues and her principal not only that she has an issue of conscience about this matter, but also that she has reasons for her concerns—reasons that have been considered by other professionals and which they have affirmed as good reasons. Hence, they are reasons that her colleagues should also respect and that they can assess. If Irene were to base her statement of conscience merely on her own experience and feelings, she has not given her coworkers any reason why they should agree with her, adopt her view, or even respect her view. Also, when Irene puts the matter in this second way, she opens it for reasoned discussion and dialogue. She announces that her sense of integrity is important to her, but also that she is open to discussion about it—not a discussion about whether she should compromise her integrity to preserve harmony, but a discussion that brings evidence, reasoning, and professional standards into the equation and that might shape her own conscience as well as that of others. She invites a collective search for the best thing to do.

Suppose, however, at the end of the day, an agreement cannot be reached. How do teachers protect their integrity when asked to do what they think is unwise or harmful? Here are a few possibilities:

1. *Accommodate the expectations of one's employer.* Is it sometimes OK to give in about a matter of conscience? We think the answer is yes. In fact, few organizations could survive or function if they were staffed by people for whom every issue was a matter of conscience and every matter of conscience was a matter of high principle where compromise was impossible. Saints are often admired from afar, but are notoriously hard to live with. Indeed, democracy requires that when we lose an argument about some policy or practice, we respect the majority view and act on it. That Irene is a good teacher who will continue to do much good and little harm (especially if she is sensitive to the possibility of harm) are reasons why she should do what she is asked to do even if it is unwise.
2. *Find productive ways to continue to press one's case.* Here we don't mean that Irene should belabor the matter at every possible opportunity. However, she might suggest that, since there is reasonable disagreement about the matter, it be reevaluated and reconsidered after a reasonable trial. That some matter has been legitimately and democratically decided does not mean that further discussion or reconsideration is barred. Irene might seek to continue the dialogue by asking that the practice be reconsidered at an appropriate time.
3. *Work around the policy.* Sometimes it is possible to comply with an unreasonable demand in a creative way so that it is turned from something harmful into something productive. Here we are not suggesting that teachers be devious, but rather that they be imaginative.

4. *Resignation.* Sometimes, if we are asked to do something that we cannot in good conscience do, and we cannot get the decision reconsidered or reversed, there is no alternative other than to quit. As noted, not every disagreement is such an occasion. Resignation is the preferred option only when we are asked to do something that violates a core moral consideration in a fundamental way or when we are asked to do something that, in our best judgment, will do serious and lasting harm. These are vague criteria, and there is no way around the fact that they involve difficult judgments.

## ETHICAL DIALOGUE

One might argue that Irene Canebrake was at fault for not trying harder to present her case to the school community. We might say, "She should have gone to the curriculum committee and tried to explain what had happened in her class" or "She was too confrontational; she did not give Angela Dormer and the school board a chance to reconsider." These observations see the problem as requiring more dialogue, not as requiring the location of sovereignty. The issue should be talked out. Why?

Consider two kinds of values that dialogue might serve. We will call these *values of community* and *values of rationality.*[12]

Dialogue often strengthens community. It can reinforce a sense of common enterprise and thereby create a sense of membership. Through dialogue *the* school can be transformed into *my* school, *its* goals into *my* goals, *its* activities into *my* activities. When decisions are achieved through dialogue, individuals who participate are more likely to own decisions and to care conscientiously for their implementation. Even when dialogue fails to achieve agreement, it may foster respect and understanding. People may be able to see the issue from the perspective of the other person and to tolerate differences when consensus is beyond reach. All of these features seem important to an organization if it is to accomplish its tasks in a purposeful and conscientious manner. They are also important features of an organization in which work is rewarding and personal relations are satisfying.

In contrast, the frequent exercise of sovereignty can degrade community. When people are motivated only by a sense of duty to obey some authority, or worse, when they feel coerced by authority, they will not do their work out of loyalty to the community, its purposes, or its members.

---

12. Much of the position we develop in this section has been inspired by the work of Jürgen Habermas on the ideal speech community and by John Dewey's insistence on the importance of community in democracy and education.

When community is broken, people are less likely to do their jobs well. Often, when educators resist treating disagreements as occasions for the exercise of sovereignty and instead seek more dialogue, they are seeking to preserve community. Dialogue also serves reasoned inquiry. It provides people with an opportunity to learn from others. They can acquire new concepts and new ways of understanding. Ideas can be subjected to criticism. Those who have special expertise can have the opportunity to share it. This social process of reflection is especially important for ethical issues. We have represented moral reflection as an attempt to express ethical intuitions in principles and to extend these principles to and test them against additional cases. We also insist that ethical reflection should be seen as a social process. There are several reasons for this. First, any process of reflection is improved when insights are shared. Second, the ethical principles that operate in a social institution must be public. They should be known and shared. This is unlikely to be the case unless they are publicly discussed and debated. Finally, dialogue about ethical issues and concepts provides the context in which the sophistication of individuals about ethical issues can be developed. We do not believe that what you have learned from this book can have an enduring effect unless the concepts that it has taught are reinforced and deepened by further conversations about ethics. Teachers are not likely to master these concepts unless they become part of conversations with fellow teachers in schools. Ethical concepts are social creations and social resources. Their vitality and sophistication are sustained by dialogue. Reflective equilibrium is as much a social affair as an individual one.

There may be an additional reason why dialogue is crucial in ethical reflection. Some ethical decisions may be validated by virtue of the fact that those who are involved agree to them. On first reflection this may seem problematic. Obviously agreement is not always a guarantee of truth. The world would not be flat even if everyone agreed that it was. Or imagine that a group of criminals agreed that it would be okay for them to rob a bank and murder all the witnesses. It does not seem reasonable to suggest that their agreement makes their robbery and murder okay.

However, the suggestion that the rightness of ethical decisions or principles is validated by agreement can be made more plausible by noting two things. First, when we engage in a process of dialogue and investigation about some such assertion as "the world is round," it seems plausible to suppose that what we are trying to do is to find out the shape of the world. The statement "the world is round" is true if, in fact, that is how the earth is shaped. But when you are reflecting about ethical issues, it is less clear that we are trying to achieve a description of reality and that our claim is true only if reality is actually that way. If ethical claims are not attempts to describe an independent reality, but rather are claims about what we should take to be fair, just, and right, then agreement among involved parties may play a different role in judging the adequacy of ethical principles and decisions.

Second, we may need to examine the nature of the agreement in our example of murder and robbery more closely. The victims of the murder and robbery were not party to the agreement. Might they have been? Can we imagine a dialogue between the robbers and their intended victims that would lead the latter to agree to being robbed and murdered? Perhaps we might. But the dialogue would be likely to have some unusual characteristics. Perhaps the victims would be coerced. They would agree because they were threatened in some way. Or perhaps they would be deceived about what they were agreeing to.

Thus not any agreement is sufficient to legitimate an ethical decision or choice. Instead, the agreement must be a consensus resulting from a dialogue that meets certain conditions. For example, the participants cannot have been coerced or deceived. Perhaps, then, any ethical decision that can validate an ethical choice must be the result of a dialogue that meets the following conditions: All of the relevant parties must be included in the discussion. The discussion must be "undominated," that is, no one should be coerced, indoctrinated, or manipulated, and everyone should be on an equal footing. No one should play a role in the discussion that can only be explained as a consequence of the exercise of power over others. The decision should be fully aired, with no relevant considerations repressed and no arguments excluded. Finally, a decision reached by such a conversation should satisfy a condition that we will call *reciprocity*. Individual participants in the decision should be able and willing to project themselves into the perspective of other parties in the discussion and to find any decision reasonable from the variety of available perspectives, not only from their own. These conditions define an *open and undominated dialogue.*

These considerations place the question of agreement in a different light. It does seem possible to think that ethical decisions are legitimated, at least in part, because they express a consensus reached by such a dialogue. That an ethical decision results from an open and undominated discussion may be a factor that actually contributes to its being a right decision. One reason for believing this is that the kind of dialogue we have been describing satisfies the principle of respect for persons. It creates conditions in which people are treated as equals. All interests are respected. Everyone's view is taken into account. People are treated as ends, not means. Thus we might view open, undominated dialogue as the principle of equal respect for persons applied to the social process of ethical deliberation.

Perhaps, then, we should resist having to choose between professionalism and democracy and instead insist on more open and undominated discussion. We have identified at least four important values that are served by open, undominated dialogue. Such dialogue helps build community; it facilitates reasoning; and it helps initiate people into the concepts and processes required for sophisticated ethical deliberation. Finally, the fact that an ethical decision emerges from an open and undominated dialogue may itself be a factor that makes the decision morally right.

This discussion has also helped us identify some of the features that make an ethical dialogue a good dialogue. We think that these features are effectively summarized by the phrase *open, undominated dialogue.* Open dialogue accepts input from all relevant participants. Moreover, it respects evidence and argument and thus does not attempt to exclude any relevant consideration from expression. Undominated dialogue avoids infecting discussion with unequal power relations. It insists that discussions respect the equal worth and the equality of interests of participants.

These ideas suggest that discussion is essential to ethical deliberation. Ethical deliberation should be thought of as a social activity conducted cooperatively. The reflective equilibrium that is sought in ethical dialogue is a social outcome. Persistent disagreement indicates that reflective equilibrium has not been achieved.

That ethical deliberation should be seen as a social and dialogical activity leads to two observations about the ethical lives of teachers in schools. We shall conclude this discussion with them. First, the character of schools in our society typically makes the ethical reflection that teachers engage in a solitary affair. Teachers work in self-contained classrooms. There are few forums in schools where it is natural to discuss ethical issues. Moreover, many schools are hierarchically structured in ways that interfere with any real dialogical process. As a consequence, teachers are unlikely to have much opportunity to engage in open and undominated ethical dialogue. If we are right about this, it is a significant shortcoming of our school systems.

Second, teachers need to be careful in how they think about their own integrity in ethical decision making. If one thinks of ethical deliberation as something one does alone, one may also think of the resulting choices in an uncompromising way. One may reason: "I achieved this decision as the result of the best moral reflection of which I am capable. It expresses my best judgment about what is right. Since I believe this choice to be the right thing to do, I am obligated to pursue it, regardless of what others may think. I cannot compromise my principles. My integrity is at stake." People who draw this conclusion run the risk of irreconcilable conflict with others who may have reflected with equal conscientiousness but reached different conclusions. Both Angela Dormer and Irene Canebrake appear to have done this. Both have taken a position from which they cannot move without sacrificing their integrity.

Sometimes ethical people have to resist compromising their integrity. However, if we recognize that ethical reflection is a social and dialogical process as well as an individual one and that one factor in the rightness of a decision is the ability to persuade others of it as the result of an undominated dialogue, we will be less likely to experience a threat to our integrity every time we find that we are in disagreement with someone else about the ethical thing to do. We will be more likely to go the extra mile in seeking consensus before we dig ourselves into a moral foxhole. Finally, we will be less likely to initiate a decision process in which the decision turns more on the question of who has sovereignty than on an open, undominated deliberative process that serves community.

## ADDITIONAL CASES

### Silence Is Not Golden

Bonnie Clyde was on the edge of a resignation. She had been the biology teacher in Millersville High for four years now and she had just gotten tenure. Thank goodness for that! Millersville was a small town in the Bible belt, a nice place full of decent, hard-working people. She loved it there, but teaching biology in the Bible belt was, if not exactly Hell, at least tough going. Evolution wasn't a popular subject in Millersville. Nobody had really twisted her arm about it. She had been taken out to lunch by some people from a local church. They had been polite and concerned. She had said that in her opinion evolution was not inconsistent with a belief in God. They had explained that even if that was true, it was inconsistent with what the Bible taught. They seemed more sad than angry that they couldn't persuade her. She suspected them of praying for her—hardly a great sin. She felt grateful to these good people. She knew they took their convictions seriously, and she knew that in other places biology teachers had been given a very hard time. Similarly, her students were polite when evolution was discussed, but most were not buying it. "Too bad," Bonnie thought. "Maybe evolution isn't essential to good living, but it's certainly essential to understanding modern biology. Evolution isn't just something most biologists believe; it's part of how they think about living things. Teaching biology without evolution is like teaching geometry by having students memorize proofs, but not trying to help them see that proofs should be consistent and that conclusions should follow from premises." At the same time, Bonnie was careful to respect her student's religious beliefs. Each time the topic came up Bonnie told her students that she did not require that they believe that evolution was true. But she did expect them to know what it was about and the role it plays in modern biology. Bonnie, her students, and the community seemed to have achieved a kind of détente. Maybe she had not gotten her students to think about biology as she knew they should, but she had been faithful to the principles of her field and had maintained her integrity in her profession.

Unfortunately, changes were in the wind. The state school board, goaded by members of the legislature, had explored various ideas about how evolution should be taught. They had rejected banning it outright, and they had rejected the idea of equal time for evolution and creationism. They knew that the Supreme Court had reviewed legislation doing these things and had found it in violation of the Establishment Clause of the First Amendment. Their current thinking was this: The state would create a fairly detailed syllabus for biology, and the state test in biology that all students must pass if they were to graduate would closely follow the syllabus. The state's curriculum would emphasize health, environmental protection, and ecology. When students finished they would know a lot about the basic food groups, the importance of recycling, and the problems caused by acid rain. Evolution would not be included in the state syllabus. Teachers would not be forbidden from teaching evolution, but they would be accountable for completing the state syllabus.

Bonnie had no idea whether writing the state's biology curriculum so as to deliberately discourage teaching evolution would prove to be illegal. But it was clear to her that she would not have time to teach evolution coherently and systematically and also cover everything in the new curriculum. Evolution would become a set of footnotes in her course, and that was not acceptable to her. None of the topics mandated by the state's new curriculum could be deeply grasped apart from an evolutionary perspective. What she was being asked to teach was not biology as biologists understood it. She was being asked to misrepresent her field to her students. How could she teach with any integrity and go along with that?

## Five Is Not Enough

The state had decided its students needed to know how to write. Moses Jones thought so, too. He had taught writing to his eighth graders for years. The state had also decided that eighth graders would be tested on their writing skills by being asked to write a five-paragraph essay for the state test. Moses was uneasy about this. Why five paragraphs? Why not three or seven? Did good writing come in just five paragraphs? He was also a little anxious about how these essays would be evaluated. Typically, when he read student writing, his comments were quite varied. He corrected spelling and grammar, but he also discussed style and helped students improve the punch and the elegance of their language. Sometime he had a lot to say about how students could improve the coherence and persuasiveness of their writing. Writing was art, logic, rhetoric, and a good deal more. He had been assured that the state would develop a rubric so that these five-paragraph essays would be judged well and judged on a consistent standard. Moses wondered if a rubric that evaluated essays with any sophistication would be too complex to allow for consistency across multiple evaluators. Any rubric that could be applied consistently would have to be simplistic. Not so, the state's testing gurus assured him. He would wait and see.

What Moses was not prepared for was the emphasis he was required to put on this five-paragraph essay in his lessons. His school was under a lot of pressure to get its students to do well on these tests. Scores were reported in the paper with comparisons to other schools, so the five-paragraph essay was to become the main focus of teaching in all the eighth-grade English classes in his district. Well, Moses decided he would just ask his students to write five-paragraph essays about the material he normally taught. The problem with this was that the state test did not ask students to write a five-paragraph essay on a story or an article they were familiar with. Instead, the students were to be given a paragraph to discuss, or they were to be asked to write about something that everyone would be able to write about—someone they were close to or where they lived, for example. How else can you put an essay in a standardized test format? Moreover, it turned out that the evaluation rubric was not much oriented to the sophistication of the argument or the stylistic qualities of the writing. Not that what it looked for was bad; students need to know how to spell and write grammatical sentences, paragraphs should be well organized, and there should be an orderly flow of ideas. But there should be a lot more—or so Moses thought.

The real problem, for Moses, was that his school insisted that practice in writing these essays be frequent and that it reflect the state test closely. This meant several essays a week were to be assigned using the state's format and that the essays were to be graded using the state's rubric. If he was going to do this, then what was he going to leave out of his own lessons to make room for the new requirements? Moses recalled an article he had read a while back about the consequences of high-stakes testing. What had the author argued? Oh yes.... It was not clear, the author had claimed, that students learned more as a result of high-stakes testing. What *was* clear was that curricular distortion and teaching to the tests were common results. He remembered the rebuttal: If the tests test for mastery of high standards, then it is a good thing if teachers align their curriculum with the standards and teach to the test. Now he knew what that meant for eighth-grade English. Perhaps this might lead to an improvement in instruction in many classrooms in the state, but he did not think it would improve his.

Moses had never disliked a number before; after all, his namesake had written a Pentateuch. But he was coming to dislike the number five. The only good thing he could find about it now was that five was the number of years he had to teach before he was fully vested in the state's retirement plan.

*Some Questions*

1.  In our commentary on teaching with integrity, we said that there were two elements that distinguished a judgment of conscience rooted in professional standards from a personal judgment. These were evidence and affirmation. Do the standards appealed to by the teachers in these two cases involve both evidence and affirmation?
2.  In each case the teacher argues that the material that he or she is asked to teach does not adequately represent the subject matter. But in no case is any teacher asked to tell a lie or deny a plain fact about the subject they teach. They are, instead, making judgments about what the purposes of their subjects are (or are not), about the standards of evidence in their fields, or about what students in their classes should be asked to know, understand, and be able to do. Are there professional standards about these matters? Consider your own area of teaching expertise. What kinds of standards are "internal" to your subject area so that you would find it a matter of conscience were you to be asked to deny them or fail to recognize them?
3.  Sometimes these things are hotly debated. Does the fact that professionals disagree mean that there are no standards of professional judgment about these matters?
4.  The case involving Angela Dormer and Irene Canebrake did not involve a disagreement about the nature of subject matter. It involved a disagreement about readiness to learn fractions. The experts about subject matter are those who engage in the practice as scholars: Physicists are the experts about physics, for example. Who are the experts about readiness? What other areas of expertise are there with respect to teaching?
5.  In each case the decisions and policies that these teachers believed threatened their professional integrity were developed democratically in that they were made by legislatures or those empowered by legislatures to make such decisions. Is the resistance of these teachers to legitimate policy undemocratic?
6.  Which of the strategies we suggested above (if any) might these teachers pursue? Are there others? Are any of these violations of professional integrity severe enough that the teacher has no choice but to resign?
7.  We have said a lot about the virtues of dialogue. Is dialogue possible in these cases? How might it be promoted?

## FOR FURTHER INQUIRY

Benjamin, Martin. "Moral Reasoning, Moral Pluralism, and the Classroom." In *Philosophy of Education 2005*, edited by Kenneth R. Howe, 23–36. Urbana, IL: Philosophy of Education Society, 2005.
    This article develops the idea of reflective equilibrium in ethics.

Gutmann, Amy, and Dennis Thompson. *Democracy and Disagreement.* Cambridge, MA: Harvard University Press, 1996.
    A statement of deliberative democracy.

Gutmann, Amy. *Democratic Education.* Princeton, NJ: Princeton University Press, 1987.
    A discussion of ethics and educational policy emphasizing the central role of deliberative democracy in educational thought.

Habermas, Jürgen. *Moral Consciousness and Communicative Action.* Cambridge, MA: MIT Press, 1900.
    A defense of "discourse ethics" that treats dialogue as central to ethical decision making.

Strike, Kenneth A. "Is Teaching a Profession: How Would We Know?" *Journal of Personnel Evaluation in Education 4* (1990): 91–117.
    A discussion of the tensions between democracy and professionalism.

Strike, Kenneth A. "Professionalism, Democracy, and Discursive Communities: Normative Reflections on Restructuring." *American Educational Research Journal 30,* no. 2 (1993): 255–75.
    This article distinguishes the Lockean tradition of democracy from deliberative democracy and applies the results to the notion of professional community.

Strike, Kenneth A. "Common Schools and Uncommon Conversations." *Journal of Philosophy of Education 41,* no. 4 (2007): 693–708.
    This article discusses the role of dialogue in dealing with three controversial issues, teaching creation science, gay rights, and teaching the Bible.

*Chapter 7*

# Conclusions and Postscript

Much of our analysis of the cases in this book was done by contrasting consequentialist and nonconsequentialist views. (This is one way, but certainly not the only way, to structure discussion about ethical dilemmas.) Is there any reason to prefer one of these orientations to the other? We have only a few brief suggestions to make. The first is that neither view is sufficient. The second is that each view to some extent makes up for the deficiencies of the other. Perhaps we should ask if they can be combined.

In our view, nonconsequentialist concepts are more fundamental. One reason for this is that they are often presupposed by consequentialist views. To see why, let us ask the following question of utilitarianism. When we are calculating the average happiness of individuals, why should we count everyone's happiness as equivalent? Perhaps some people are inherently more worthwhile than others and, thus, their happiness should count more. In calculating the average utility we should multiply the happiness of individuals by a factor reflecting their intrinsic worth. To explain why this suggestion is offensive, we will quickly be led to nonconsequentialist concepts such as equal respect for persons, impartiality, and universality.

The chief difficulty with nonconsequentialist views is that they cannot be coherently applied without a knowledge of what is good for human beings and of how actions affect the welfare of others. Perhaps the average utility principle does not capture well the idea of respect for persons. If that is true, then the conclusion to draw is that we need other principles that show us how to decide what kinds of consequences do capture the idea of equal respect. A viable ethical theory will embed a concern for consequences within a framework of nonconsequentialist ideals.

We conclude with a comment on a consideration that has been a substantial motivating factor behind the approach of this book. We have spent a good deal of time discussing ethical relativism and contrasting consequentialist and nonconsequentialist views. We have done this because we believe that understanding them makes a difference not only in how teachers ought to behave toward students, but in our basic understanding of what education is about.

Socrates is recorded as saying that the unexamined life is not worth living. Why not? In our view, the point of this maxim is that to fail to reflect on how one lives is to fail to recognize one's status as a moral agent. It is to refuse to accept responsibility for one's self. In a fundamental way, it is to refuse to be a person.

We have been unhappy with utilitarianism because it is happiness, not growth as persons, that is the first concern for utilitarians. Growth must be a contingent value and subservient to happiness. We have been unhappy with relativism because it destroys the point of moral growth, as it destroys the point of everything.

In our view, the compelling matter is growth as a moral agent, as someone who cares about others and is willing and able to accept responsibility for one's self, as someone who can engage in open, undominated dialogue with others about a common life and accept shared responsibility for the group's life. Promoting this kind of development is what teachers ought to be fundamentally about, whatever else it is that they are about. We are first and foremost in the business of creating persons. It is our first duty to respect the dignity and value of our students and to help them to achieve their status as free, rational, and feeling moral agents.

It has been traditional to inscribe profound maxims over the entrances of schools. Our suggestion for what ought to be there is contributed by Dr. Seuss. "A person's a person no matter how small."

## POSTSCRIPT

Professors Strike and Soltis have gone to lunch with several students and a colleague from the philosophy department. The students have just finished *The Ethics of Teaching*. Both the philosopher and the students seem bothered by the book. The following conversation results.

*Student 1:* When I went home on break, I took your book with me, and my father looked through it. He is quite unhappy with it. He says that ethics cannot be discussed apart from religion and that he suspects you two of being secular humanists. I don't want to go that far, but it does seem to me that my religious training is a part of my ethical outlook. I have a hard time thinking about ethics apart from it.

*Student 2:* It never occurred to me to think of you guys as secular humanists. But it does seem to me that you've left a lot out. I've been reading a couple of feminist authors. They talk a lot about caring, and they have argued that the kind of ethics you guys write about is male ethics. Shouldn't the ethics of education have something to say about teachers caring about students?

*Philosopher:* Not only have you two ignored religion and caring—you've ignored most of the history of philosophy! You write as if the only philosophers who have ever existed are Kant and a few utilitarians. How about Aristotle or Plato or Dewey? They've all had some rather profound things to say about both ethics and education. How come no mention of them?

*Strike:* (looking distinctly uncomfortable) Um ... ah ... Well at least I'm fairly sure I'm not a secular humanist. Actually I'm a Presbyterian. But I do have to admit that the view of ethics we present is quite secular and that Kant and utilitarianism figure centrally in the text. However, this text is written for use by prospective teachers who may hold various religious beliefs or none, and who will have to teach in public schools. There are some obvious problems in trying to teach ethics from a religious position if the ethics is for public institutions. If ethics can't be separated from religion in some way, it's hard to see how we could talk about ethics in public contexts without violating someone's freedom of religion.

*Soltis:* (looking his usual confident self) Perhaps Plato might help us understand why ethics must be independent of religion. Plato wrote a dialogue entitled *Euthyphro* in which he discusses the nature of piety. I can suggest an argument that is not quite Plato's but has much in common with it. Suppose someone said that right actions are those actions commanded or willed by God. A modern Socrates (Plato's voice in his dialogues) might ask how it is that God always commands that which is right. There are two answers, neither of which is very satisfactory. One is that right is whatever it is that God commands us to do and wrong is whatever God forbids. But if that were true, God might command murder and that would make murder right, or He might forbid kindness and that would make kindness evil.

*Student 1:* But I never believed that God just went around arbitrarily commanding and forbidding things. I always assumed that He was righteous and good, and therefore He would only command things that were themselves righteous and good.

*Soltis:* That, of course, is the other alternative. Actions are not right because God commands them. Instead, God commands them because they are right. But while this has the advantage of not making God seem arbitrary in His dealings with people, it also suggests that the difference between what is right and wrong is not dependent on God's will. If God commands that which is right because it is right, then there must be something that makes it right independently of God's willing it. In this way God doesn't seem very different from a wise and just human ruler. He commands what is just because it is just. However, the standard of rightness or justice must be independent of the fact that it is commanded. If that's so, we should be able to say what makes something right or wrong without having to decide if God has willed it.

*Philosopher:* Yes, yes. But you know it's more complicated than that. For example some theologians have held that God's commands express His nature, not His will. Plato's argument (or your version of it) doesn't seem as successful against that view.

*Strike:* Actually, I've always thought that what made theological ethics interesting had little to do with all this stuff about God's commands. It seems to me that what is important is that theological ethics has some distinctive ethical concepts that are not often included in secular ethics. I think such concepts as reconciliation and redemption are quite important even apart from talk about God. One might argue that a major part of religious ethics is about restoring relationships.

*Student 2:* That might even have a place for caring?

*Strike:* I would think so.

*Philosopher:* Well, I'm sure that's very nice, but poor Aristotle and Dewey are still out in the cold. And you certainly didn't have much to say about caring, redemption, and reconciliation in your book. Aristotle has a great deal to say about the development of character that's worth listening to, and Dewey has much to say about the philosophy of education.

*Strike:* I've always been impressed by Aristotle's views on character formation.

*Soltis:* And I have high regard for Dewey's educational theories.

*Student 2:* Well, if Professor Strike is big on relationships and Aristotle, and Professor Soltis likes Dewey's views on education, why doesn't any of this come out in the book?

*Strike:* One reason is that we don't see ourselves as answering questions like "What is the nature of a good life?" or "What is the nature of a good education?" We think of ourselves as addressing questions about how people who might disagree deeply about these things can cooperate and settle disputes in public institutions.

*Student 1:* I'm confused. Why, for example, would this lead you to ignore God?

*Strike:* Suppose that you and an atheist had to work together on some common project, perhaps providing an education for your children, and that you had to agree on some basis for your cooperation. How would you feel if the atheist insisted that atheism had to be part of the basis for your cooperation?

*Student 1:* Obviously I wouldn't like that. I'd refuse to cooperate.

*Philosopher:* And would you insist instead that the atheist accept your theism as a basis for your cooperation?

*Student 1:* Well, that doesn't really seem fair, although I do think he'd be better off if he agreed with me. I suppose, however, that if he isn't allowed to insist on his atheism, to be consistent, I can't insist that he agree with my theism.

*Strike:* If you can't insist on your theism, and he can't insist on his atheism, how would you find a basis for cooperation?

*Student 1:* Well, I suppose we would have to agree to treat our religious differences as private matters to be pursued outside of schools.

*Student 2:* And I suppose that we would have to discover some ethical concepts that we can agree on even though we disagree about religious convictions.

*Philosopher:* You might consider that if you insist on thinking this way about your "ethics for public institutions" you will have to discover ethical principles that are neutral to a great deal more than religion. They may have to be neutral to most fully articulated views about a good life, and they might even have to be neutral to conflicting conceptions of a good education. After all, a lot of people who may want to cooperate in public institutions will disagree about such matters too.

*Strike:* I think that's basically right. The "public ethic" for a pluralistic society has to be neutral to a lot of important things. Its view of a good life and a good education will be a bit thin. That doesn't mean that "thicker" views about the best ways to live and about a good education aren't important. What it means is that, in a free society, we can't impose them.

*Student 2:* So what kinds of ethical concepts can people agree on even though they disagree deeply about such important matters?

*Soltis:* They have mostly to do with what is just or fair. I suppose that the ethical principles we talk about in this book would be good examples. Ideas such as free speech, due process, privacy, or democratic decision making seem the kinds of things that people who disagree about much might agree on as ways to cooperate fairly. For example, I'd be surprised if there's any special reason why theists and atheists would have to disagree about due process.

*Student 2:* But how about character development or relationships such as caring? Professor Strike seems to think that these are important to a well-considered ethic, but you don't say much about them.

*Soltis:* I agree with Professor Strike that these are important topics. In fact, I think they are important for the ethics of teaching. Teachers should be people of good character, and they should care about their students. At the same time, character and a capacity to care seem to us to be things that develop over a lifetime, and they are not primarily cognitive. It's not easy for me to see how we can reform people's character or turn them into caring people in a short book. But we do think we can help them understand what free speech and due process are about and how to think about ethics rationally so they may reach public decisions that are discussable and defensible.

*Student 2:* But you sound as if this "public ethic" of fairness and justice you talk about and an ethic of relationships are perfectly compatible. Don't some people treat them as alternatives?

*Strike:* It's true that some writers sound as though these views are opposed. But I don't quite see it that way.

*Philosopher:* And how do you see it?

*Strike:* It seems to me that an ethic of caring or other ethics to which relationships are central try to describe what human relationships are ideally like. Relationships such as love, or caring, or friendship are very important to the quality of people's lives. Moreover, in some contexts it is important that these relationships should be the central concern. Where they are, there is little need to worry about justice or about working out rules that detail the basis of cooperation. In families where people love each other and care about each other, there's often little need for discussion of fairness or justice. In fact, when friends or family members spend a lot of time worrying about fairness, that can be a sign that the friendship or the caring relationship is at risk.

*Student 2:* So you see justice as important in places where caring cannot be taken for granted?

*Strike:* That's right. Maybe in an ideal world human relations would be governed by friendship, love, or caring. But the world isn't always perfect. Moreover, many who have written about caring or friendship have emphasized that these are relationships that we have with particular people. We can't be friends with everyone, and we can't care for everyone. We have to decide how we can relate responsibly to those for whom we do not care. Another way to put it is that friendship and caring express ways to relate that people have found to be good and worthwhile ways to connect with some people. Justice tells us how we must relate to people however we feel about them and regardless of whether we care for them. The "public ethic" sets minimum standards. It's a kind of moral safety net.

*Philosopher:* Well, all of this seems doubtful to me, but at least I begin to get a clearer picture of why you included what you included and omitted what you omitted from this book. But why all this stuff about consequentialist and nonconsequentialist ethics?

*Soltis:* We did this because these two broad groups of ethical theories have historically been major ways in which philosophers have sought to justify various aspects of justice. Certainly anyone who grasps these arguments will have made a good start at understanding how philosophers have thought about the kinds of moral concepts that govern social cooperation in liberal democratic societies that respect pluralism, although there is much more to be learned.

*Philosopher:* But I have noticed that Professor Soltis grows silent when Professor Strike waxes eloquent about neutrality between differing conceptions of a good life.

*Soltis:* Hmm. Yes, sometimes I think Ken gets carried away here. I wonder if a viable educational system might not require a "'thicker" conception of a good life than he will allow. There are also a few other things he's said that I'd like to repair.

*Strike:* Indeed, fine fellow and profound thinker though he is, I'm not entirely certain that Jonas has fully seen the light on several topics. Even worse, I change my mind on some of them two or three times a year.

*Philosopher:* So even though you two agree on enough to write a book, if I really probed your views deeply I might find some fundamental disagreements down there?

*Strike:* Could be. But we think the most important lesson of this book is that even when people disagree, even deeply, about the justification of ethical concepts, it's still possible for them to agree on some basic rules for what it means to treat people fairly.

*Soltis:* Actually, while I think that's an important observation, I think that the most important lesson of this book is that dialogue and reflection are required if people are to make progress on some difficult and important questions. No doubt my colleague and coauthor also has much respect for dialogue and reflection.

*Strike:* No doubt.

*Philosopher:* But to all dialogue there must come an end. I suggest that we devote our remaining moments to deciding who should pick up the tab for lunch. I think that since Professor Strike invited us to this conversation, he should repress his natural predilections to frugality and pick up the check.

Professor Strike, feeling some pain at the suggestion and silently asking the forgiveness of his Scottish ancestors, but noting the relieved looks on the students' faces and recalling that Professor Soltis paid the last time, picks up the bill and walks toward the cash register thinking ambiguous thoughts about the necessity of fairness.

# Chapter 8

# Supplemental Case Studies

The cases we have considered thus far were designed to illustrate moral issues and to get you to think about basic ideas regarding the ethics of teaching. Real-world ethical situations, however, do not just illustrate and provide food for thought—they require decision and action. As a moral person operating in the complex real world, you will need to identify legitimate moral interests and rights of others. As an educator, this means not only those of your students, but also of professional colleagues and staff, parents, and others. This requires the ability to empathize, to put yourself in another's place. You will also need to chart a reasonable course of action based on moral concepts and consequences that do the most good or least harm or uphold important principles. Sometimes you will even be called upon to justify your decisions and actions.

Of course, not all the instances of moral decision making and action that you will face will be emergencies or life threatening or challenged by others. In our daily dealings with people, we are always in a state of potential ethical relationship with each other in simple as well as complex and difficult ways. Part of what we hope to accomplish with this book is to sensitize you to that ever-present moral potential in human situations and to dispose you to treat it responsibly whenever you recognize it. Sometimes this will mean no more than showing respect for persons, for their privacy, or for equity. Sometimes it will require deeper reflection, searching analysis, careful judgment, and tactful action. Sometimes it will help if you share your thoughts, feelings, and reasons with others as you seek reflective equilibrium and your own moral growth as a person and as a professional.

Obviously, we cannot present the real world to you in this chapter, but we can provide a number of unanalyzed cases that touch on a broad range of moral concepts and potential consequences for you to think about. This will give you some practice in ethical thinking and theorizing as well as provide you with an opportunity to try to use some of the things you learned in this book. Ideally, these cases should be discussed with others. We have tried to make them the "next best thing" to real-world situations that can and do occur in everyday teaching situations. Most have been drawn from the experiences of practicing teachers.

Remember as you deal with these cases that part of what we have argued with regard to ethical objectivity is that ethical decision making is not just following the rules or applying the right moral principle and sticking to it no matter what. Considering the context, using your moral intuition to search for relevant underlying moral feelings, concepts, and principles, testing them and considering the present state of your moral theory and the rights, interests, feelings, and reasons of others-all may be necessary to reach a justifiable decision about a moral course of action.

Discussing these cases with others will give you an opportunity to think out loud and to hear others do so while the group tries objectively and rationally to reach a provisionally valid agreement in ethics. We think you will be surprised at the agreements reached regarding moral intuitions and the willingness of people not only to hear and respect others' views but also to accept good reasons for changing their own. This should be done not to reach consensus for its own sake, but to reach the most morally acceptable decision under the circumstances. Of course, there will be some disagreements and unsettled cases. The world is not neat and simple. Objective and rational discussion in moral matters offers no guarantee of successful reflective equilibrium in every case, but it does offer more promise for moral growth and moral sensitivity than does a relativistic policy of "to each his own."

The following procedures and suggestions may be helpful to you as you prepare to discuss the cases and do your own analyses. They should not be looked on as a recipe for reaching moral decisions. There are no such recipes. You will, of course, need to use your moral intuitions, consider consequences, empathize, search for alternatives, be reasonable and sincere. But there is no special or magical order for doing these things that will guarantee success. Creative ethical thinking needs to be cultivated by doing it with the proper attitudes and persistence.

1. Read a case through once quickly and reach a "seat of the pants" teacher decision in the case. Ask yourself what moral concept(s) or principle(s) or consequence(s) would explain and justify your decision as the teacher.
2. Reread the case and try to put yourself in the position of other major actors in the case. Playing those roles, do you see any legitimate claims or rights or ethical principles that might be advanced by the other persons in the case that might give you good reasons to alter your decision?
3. Reconsider the case from the point of view of the teacher. What central or basic moral concept(s) is (are) operative? Can you construct a consequentialist and a nonconsequentialist argument? Which appears stron-

ger? Why? Can they work together? Do thought experiments with examples.
4. Discuss the case with others. Test your position with them. Be open to
   their ideas and reasons but be true to what you honestly consider to be
   the most compellingly reasonable moral position, yours or theirs, as it
   develops. Can a reflective equilibrium consensus on moral theory or
   principle be reached? Remember, the point of considering these cases is
   not just the practical one of solving a problem, but also being ethical in
   its solution and continuing your own development as a moral person.
   If consensus is reached, is it an accident of the similarity of the people
   in the room or is there reason to believe others would agree? Can you
   think of a plausible objection? Can you imagine how a person quite different from you might respond? If no consensus develops, can you find
   the basic points at issue? Are they always bound to be in conflict? What
   different moral theories do they lead to?

There is no end to the questions you can ask and think about regarding
these cases as you explore and, we hope, become more sensitive to the ethics of teaching. It will probably be impossible for you and your class to examine and discuss all the cases in this chapter in the fullness required by
an objective and rational approach. To assist you in selecting cases of interest and to give you an overview of what each is about, we have provided a
schematic summary in table 1 at the end of this section. In it we have identified the case by its title and the topic it treats, the pages it appears on, and
the central moral concepts or principles at issue. We hope that the cases in
this chapter will challenge your thinking and develop your ethical sensitivities as educators and as moral persons.

You may find that a case can be made more realistic by having others
assume the roles of the various individuals described in the case. Of course,
you may wish to write and share your own cases based on personal experience. These are often the most realistic.

If you do decide to try writing your own cases, the following suggestions may be helpful:

1. It is best, and easiest, if you write about those matters with which you
   are familiar, issues that you have encountered in your own professional
   experience. Personal experience, observation, and analysis make it possible to write a realistic and meaningful case.
2. Try to present a problem that is encountered in teaching, and, through
   the case, make reference to underlying ethical issues. The case must
   have an issue, and you the writer must have a purpose. The case's purpose, its pedagogical objective, provides the writer with direction and
   guidance during the telling of the story.

3. The problem must be difficult, an ambiguous situation that is in need of decision and justification. Questions should not be too leading, rigid, or exhaustive, but should allow the reader some spontaneity and free-

**Table 2.** Summary of Cases and Disputes

| Page | Title | Topic |
|------|-------|-------|
| 143 | "Teacher Burnout"<br>An alchoholic colleague | Loyalities, obligation to educate, whistle blowing, equity |
| 145 | "Whose Rights: Students' or Parents'?"<br>Abortion | Life, parents' rights, students' welfare, privacy, maturity |
| 147 | "You Get What You Pay For"<br>Cut in funds, teacher gives advance placement class in home | Students' welfare, obligation to fellow teachers and teacher organizations |
| 149 | "Pledge of Allegiance"<br>Self-confessed rule breaker, marijuana | Confidentiality, privacy, responsibility for enforcing school rules |
| 150 | "Teacher or Friend?"<br>Students invited to parties at teacher's home | Professional and personal domains |
| 151<br>153<br><br>153 | "Professional Conduct: Two Cases"<br>  1. Students seek teachers' appraisal of principal and school policies<br>  2. Teacher reconsiders a team-teaching agreement | Professional relations, surveillance, agreements, due process |
| 154 | "College or Workforce?"<br>Students put in vocational track; parents want college prep | Parents' and students' rights, professional judgment and consequences |
| 156 | "Values Clarification"<br>Personal-values course questioned by parents | Teacher autonomy, parents' rights, teaching values |
| 158 | "Abuse? Neglect? or Nothing to Worry About?"<br>A teacher suspects child abuse | Child abuse, child neglect, physical punishment, parental rights |
| 160 | "Friendly Support or Sexual Harassment?"<br>Teacher–supervisor relations | Sexual harassment, normal human relations |
| 161 | "Grading Policies"<br>Three teachers with three different ways of grading | Fairness, professional autonomy |

dom of interpretation. Sometimes it is useful to make reference to more general issues that are embedded in the case.

4.  In the actual writing of the case, it is necessary to set the scene. The first paragraph ordinarily describes the situation within which the story develops, and successive paragraphs introduce characters, their actions and points of view. Often these points of view are incompatible, but it is important that you make it possible for the reader to empathize with each character. The problem is developed and presented through the course of events that are reported by the writer until the moment of conflict or decision. Be sure to develop competing justifications for the conflicting points of view. End with some relevant questions or alternative courses of action that the reader might consider.

5.  Reread your case as if you were someone else looking at it for the first time. Are the issues and facts clear? Do you feel that you have accomplished your original pedagogical objective? Revise, if necessary.

## TEACHER BURNOUT

Michael Baker was a recent appointee to the history faculty at Woodrow Wilson Senior High School. He had been a good student in college and had done well as a student teacher, but he had many doubts about his preparedness for his new job. He was not an experienced teacher, and the real life of the classroom had not been fully described in his teaching manual. Michael wished that there was someone to whom he could speak about the daily problems and tasks of a high-school teacher. He needed a mentor.

He found a mentor, and a friend, in Frank Thompson. Mr. Thompson had taught history at Woodrow Wilson for twelve years, and he was thought to be an excellent teacher. He was a favorite with the student body, his classes were lively, and his students' scores in statewide examinations compared favorably with history scores at other schools.

Frank Thompson was willing to share his experience as a teacher. After work, over beers, he would regale Michael with stories of life at the school. Before long, Michael came to know the idiosyncracies and humors of his fellow teachers and even a bit of gossip about the students. Frank's information and support helped Michael to feel more comfortable in his work. Michael did not care to drink as much as Frank, but the occasional hangover was not too great a price to pay for the pleasant company and the tips on teaching.

Sometimes Frank would overdo the afterwork tippling, and it showed in his eyes the next morning. Occasionally, Mike would cover one of

Frank's classes in his free time, while Frank recuperated over coffee in the faculty lounge. He did not mind doing a favor for a friend, and he thought that some exposure to Frank's classes would be a good experience for him. These students usually tested among the best in the history exam, and Michael wanted to find out why. Frank told him that he rarely used a planned lecture and that it would be good for Michael to take the plunge and trust his instincts in the classroom. The students worked hard, and they deserved a little fresh air.

Michael discovered that trusting his instincts was no guarantee of success. He probed the class with several questions on recent American history in order to get some idea of the state of their knowledge. However, most of the class did not respond, and those few answers he elicited were often wrong or irrelevant. Finally, out of exasperation, he asked the class what they ordinarily did with Mr. Thompson. He was told that the class usually spent most of the time talking about current events, television, and sports. In that case, asked Mr. Baker, how were they going to prepare for tests and the statewide examination? The students told him that Mr. Thompson always gave them a list of questions to study in preparation for tests. These questions, or some variations, were usually on the tests, and the students who prepared scored well. Mr. Thompson had promised that he would do the same for the statewide examination and, in fact, had already started preparing them in the same manner.

Michael was very disturbed by what he had been told in that class. The students did not seem to learn very much history. Rather, they had been shepherded through a series of tests in such a way that they would grade well. Now, they were being coached for the state examinations. This did not seem right, and Michael decided to ask Frank Thompson about the situation.

Frank had recuperated, but he was still irritable. He was very blunt in his response. Mike's problem, he said, simply did not matter. Frank had learned a while ago that his work did not make that much difference in the lives of his students, and it was not making him very happy either. If Bozo the Clown were in front of the classroom, the results would be the same. The bright kids would do well, the dummies would fare poorly, and his efforts would not change the outcome very much. So, he had decided, why not make the whole process as painless as possible? Frank tried to make his time in the classroom pleasant, and he hoped that it would not interfere with his evenings. He provided his students interesting conversation and cursory instruction in the subject. If they were able to answer the series of questions that they had been given before the tests, he was satisfied, the students were satisfied, and no one was wiser. In the case of the state examination, he had a file of old exams that he used to prime the students for good performances. If necessary, with a few phone calls to various sources, he could find out what the trends were in the current test. If the students scored well with his help, he would be satisfied that he had done his job well, for grades were the bottom line that made him and the school look good. This is what he did, and he would continue to follow this procedure until that wonderful day when he qualified for a pension and could leave teaching. He told Mike Baker that it was none of his business.

Michael felt that it was his business, but he did not know what to do about his friend. Frank was in bad shape. He drank too much, neglected his duties, and the students were not being served adequately. Michael felt that he should tell someone.

*Some Questions*

1. Friendships and professional relationships are based on mutual trust, loyalty, and, among other things, respect. In this case, Michael has had his belief in these principles stretched to the breaking point. Do you think he has good reason to "blow the whistle" on Frank, to tell appropriate superiors about what is going on?
2. Has Frank done anything wrong? He does not drink in school or arrive drunk. He teaches to the test, but many teachers do that. Moreover, state standardized tests are given to ensure equity of evaluation across different schools and districts. One could argue that Frank is doing the right thing. Are Frank's students being educated?
3. How might the principles of benefit maximization and respect for persons apply in this case?

## WHOSE RIGHTS: STUDENTS' OR PARENTS'?

Lydia Simpson taught physical education and health education at a suburban high school. She had graduated from college a few years before and, while at school, had been active in intercollegiate athletics and various feminist groups. Lydia was young enough to remember clearly the confusion of adolescence, yet mature and able to speak of those decisions that mark our growth as adults. As a teacher, she attempted to imbue her students with a sense of self-worth and a knowledge of the opportunities that could be theirs as women in the modern world. As an adviser, she lent a sympathetic ear to her students' problems and aspirations. The girls saw her as a person worthy of emulation, and they responded to her concern in kind. Those bonds of mutual respect and affection, which can be among the greatest joys for a teacher, grew between Lydia and many of her students, extending beyond the confines of the school.

As a health educator and feminist, Lydia was determined that her charges become aware of their reproductive rights and responsibilities, for she knew that they would face difficult and complicated decisions about sexual behavior. In Lydia's classes, sex education was a matter of values clarification, as well as biology and human anatomy. In addition to detailed instruction in the facts of sexual life, the students discussed a variety of adult sexual practices and a number of related ethical views about these activities. Lydia emphasized that young men and women have several options they can pursue: celibacy, different forms of birth control, and, in unfortunate cases, abortion. Lydia attempted to make it clear to her students that, because their bodies and their futures were at issue, they had the right to make these decisions. In order that she not infringe upon their rights or stray from her obligations as a teacher, Lydia was careful that she offer a balanced presentation and not seem to espouse any one view. She hoped that her instruction and advice would be of some benefit and that all would work out well for her students in this sensitive area of life.

Things do not always work out well. A junior girl named Karen, one of Lydia's favorites, came to her one day in a very distressed state. Karen was pregnant, or at least thought that she was pregnant, for she was afraid to speak to her family doctor. She was also afraid to speak to her parents, who were quite religious and had tried to be strict with her. For this reason, she had been slow to approach them on the subject of birth control, and the results of her unguided experimentation had been unfortunate. She needed Lydia's help. Would she, Karen asked, take her to a clinic and, if necessary, advise her about an abortion?

Lydia was stunned, and she was confused about the proper course of action to follow. Several contradictory principles and emotions seemed to collide in the girl's question. As an independent-minded person and a feminist, Lydia felt that any woman as young as Karen could not sacrifice her present and future happiness because of one mistake. Abortion seemed to be the most likely alternative. However, as an educator, Lydia might not have the right to interject her opinion and active support into this sensitive situation. Some people, particularly Karen's parents, would consider this being party to a murder. Lydia realized that while Karen might have some rights concerning her future and reproductive freedom, her parents also had rights and an obligation to nurture and provide moral guidance for their daughter. Did Karen's right to privacy and freedom of action outweigh considerations of parental authority and parental right to know about the behavior of a minor? Lydia wished that there were one course of action or advice she could recommend that would balance these competing imperatives and still resolve the dilemma.

*Some Questions*

1. Respect for persons is a very fundamental ethical principle. Often, in debates over abortion, a pro or con position is based on claims about when or whether a fetus is a person. In this case, Karen and her parents are also candidates for respect as persons. Can you construct an argument for Karen's rights and for her parents' rights? Which would take precedence in this case? Why?

2. Lydia must weigh a number of obligations and potential consequences before she reaches a decision about taking Karen to a clinic. List as many of these as possible. In this case, which of these weighs most heavily and why? What would you decide to do if you were Lydia?

## YOU GET WHAT YOU PAY FOR

In 1980, following in the footsteps of their forebears who organized the Boston Tea Party, the residents of Massachusetts once again rose up in protest against what they perceived to be burdensome taxation. Rather than dumping anything into Boston harbor this time, however, the citizens voted for a measure called Proposition 2½, which put limits on the ability of cities and towns in the state to assess property taxes. The subsequent loss in revenue forced the curtailment of municipal services of all kinds-police and fire departments were reduced, refuse collection was eliminated. Particularly hard hit were the public-school systems, where enrichment and other special programs, extracurricular activities, and sports were severely reduced or eliminated entirely.

Marshbury High School, a suburban school with a student body of approximately 1,200, had always enjoyed a reputation as one of the best public high schools in the state. Each year a large percentage of the graduating class had gone on to college, many of the students attending Ivy League and similarly selective schools. With the advent of Proposition 2½ and its consequences, however, the school had to lay off teachers and eliminate programs. Advanced Placement and enrichment programs as well as special education and sports had all gotten the axe. Those teachers in the system who were lucky enough to retain their jobs had responded to the treatment of their colleagues with a "rulebook slowdown." The taxpayers would get what they paid for and not a bit more.

Jerrold Ross, head of the history department, had been a popular and well-respected teacher in the system for nearly twenty years. He had always taken an exceptional interest in his students, especially the bright ones, and many of them had stayed in touch with him through college and beyond. Of all the bright students he had had over the years, however, the juniors in the AP history class this year were the best. He had taught them when they were sophomores and he had been looking forward to having them again as seniors. But because Proposition 2½ had forced the elimination of the AP program for the next year, these students would be part of his standard American history class with an enrollment of over 40.

Mr. Ross is not happy with this situation. He thinks the taxpayers were stupid to have voted the measure and shares his colleagues' disdain for them. But he does not feel, as they apparently do, that the children should suffer for the sins of their parents. Mr. Ross has decided to teach the AP curriculum to the kids who would have been in the class on his own time, in his own home. The students are enthusiastic, but the other teachers are not. They feel that Mr. Ross's decision shows callous disregard for the teachers who have lost their jobs and they are pressuring him to call off his plans for the independent effort. As a result, Mr. Ross has had a moment or two of doubt. Is he playing right into the hands of the shortsighted taxpayers? To whom does he owe the greatest allegiance-his students or his colleagues?

*Some Questions*

1. Mr. Ross is caught between his obligations to his students and to his fellow teachers. Arguments based on respect for persons and benefit maximization could be constructed to support either side. Are there other factors in this case that might give more weight to one group, students or fellow teachers, than the other?
2. Role-play a meeting at which Mr. Ross, one of his AP students, a laid-off teacher, a citizen who supports Proposition 2½, a parent of an AP and a non-AP student, and a teachers' union representative testify before the school board. What principles are at issue? Should the school board allow Mr. Ross to teach in his home? Do they have a right to tell Mr. Ross what he can do on his own time? Does the teachers' union have any claim on limiting Mr. Ross's end run on their "rulebook slowdown" stance?
3. Is this a case of democracy at work? What does that mean in a public-school setting? Where does authority reside? How can changes be brought about democratically?

# PLEDGE OF ALLEGIANCE

Morningside Academy, a coeducational day school for 500 students in grades 7 through 12, was founded in 1904, in part for the purpose of helping "students to make their own decisions, assume responsibility for their choices, and respond sensitively to the needs of others." In recent years, under the stewardship of Headmaster Robert Jennings, the school has embodied a staunchly conservative philosophy of education.

One area of student life that reflects this philosophy concerns the use of drugs and alcohol by students. As headmaster, Mr. Jennings has taken an unequivocal stand against the use of these substances and has clearly articulated this position to both faculty and student constituencies. It is understood that a violation of this major school rule will result in immediate expulsion from the academy. Recently, for example, several popular seniors were expelled from Morningside when, a week before graduation, a night watchman discovered them drinking from a small flask in the locker room after the Spring Sports Banquet. In small-group meetings with advisers the next day, students were reminded of the academy's policy.

The adviser system is thought by students, parents, and school administration to enhance the goals of the academy through friendly and supportive interaction and dialogue. Ginny, an eighth-grade student, has scheduled an appointment for the third time this week with her adviser, Mr. Stimson, having broken two previous appointments. During the meeting, she seems on edge and unfocused, though clearly anxious to talk about something. Toward the close of their disjointed conference, Ginny ultimately confesses that on two occasions in recent weeks she and another student have slipped behind the academic building to try marijuana. Upon further questioning, Ginny admits that it was "fun," but that she is afraid she might do it again. Apparently she is worried about being caught and having to suffer the consequences, which, she clearly understands, include expulsion from Morningside. Will Mr. Stimson please help her, Ginny implores, as she, late for her next class, rushes out of his office. Aside from chewing gum in study hall, a minor infraction of the rules, Ginny is on High Honor Roll with an A- average. Ginny is Headmaster Jennings's youngest daughter.

Mr. Stimson, in his second year of teaching and coaching at Morningside Academy, finds himself in a quandary, puzzled by how to respond to his advisee's confession. Should he go to the school's administration with this information, Mr. Stimson will have broken the bond of trust that allowed Ginny to discuss her situation in confidence in the first place. And if the school authorities become involved, Ginny most likely will be expelled from Morningside Academy for her confessed misbehavior.

And yet, Mr. Stimson's two-year probationary period is over at the end of this school year and he faces an administrative evaluation for the renewal of his contract. Should Ginny be caught smoking marijuana on campus, he worries, and school officers discover that he had prior knowledge of Ginny's activities without bringing them to their attention, his professional conduct would be in serious question and his contract in jeopardy. That Ginny is Headmaster Jennings's daughter only compounds the dilemma.

*Some Questions*

1. This is a case of mixed obligations. One is to a student who has assumed a confidential relationship and the other is to being responsible for following school rules. Which should take precedence here? Why?
2. There is also an important dimension of self-interest and prudence in this case. Clearly it is not wrong to consider one's own well-being in addition to the well-being of others. If you were Mr. Stimson, how might you try to protect yourself in this situation? Could you do this ethically? On what grounds would you defend your action?

## TEACHER OR FRIEND?

Block City is a small factory town in upstate New York that is noted for its tool-and-die industry. The families who live in Block City are second- and third-generation Americans who take pride in their accomplishments and the sort of life they have carved out in the town. A significant source of civic pride is Block City High School, which has established a reputation for having one of the best scholastic football teams in the country. The students who play on the varsity football team enjoy the popularity and prominence that accompanies the team's achievements. They hold a special position in the social life of the town, because both their peers and adult fans, of which there are many, hold them in great esteem.

Ron Nelson, the coach of the football team, is a young, good-looking twenty-seven-year-old who was hired the year he graduated from college. Mr. Nelson is an alumnus of Block City, and he was an all-star halfback on the varsity football team throughout his high school career. During his tenure as coach he has upheld the winning tradition at the school. Mr. Nelson is a very enthusiastic coach, and he has good rapport with many of the students. They often seek his advice on a variety of problems that range from grades to girlfriends. Mr. Nelson also helps junior and senior football players select colleges and athletic programs, and many Block City footballers have received scholarships to well-known universities.

During the past year, a select group of football players, known as the "inner circle," has become very close to Mr. Nelson. They often spend Saturdays and some weeknights at his home, watching football games on television or simply hanging around socializing. To be invited to Coach Nelson's gatherings gives a student a certain extra bit of status at the school.

There has been some talk in the administration and among some of the faculty about the propriety of Mr. Nelson's relationship with these students. Rumors have indicated that beer drinking and raucous parties take place at his house when the students are there. Nobody has approached Mr. Nelson, and he ignores the rumors.

Mr. Nelson has planned another party for a weekend in early December in order to mark the conclusion of another successful football season. It will be a reunion for some of his old football buddies, many of whom now recruit or coach for university teams. He has invited the better players on the team, and they cannot wait to go. It will be fun, and they will be able to meet some people who will be able to further their football careers.

Word of this party has caused some dispute at the school. Some faculty members have approached the principal, saying that it was unprofessional of Mr. Nelson to invite these students to a party of this sort. Alcoholic beverages would be served, and the players were not old enough to drink. It is not unlikely that the party will get out of hand. These faculty members have demanded that the principal reprimand Mr. Nelson and have him withdraw his invitation to the students. Others feel that the idea for a party is harmless and may allow some of the players to make some helpful contacts. Besides, it is not anyone's business what the coach and his players do outside of school.

*Some Questions*

1. Where does the private behavior of teachers start and the professional domain for which they are publicly accountable end?
2. If Mr. Nelson had been working on the side as a talent scout for the state university's football coach, would this significantly alter the case? Why or why not?
3. Can you think of things we ordinarily take to be private or personal matters that a teacher might be held accountable for to a school principal or school board? What would be the grounds for making such claims?

## PROFESSIONAL CONDUCT: TWO CASES

Janet Wyler had taught history for several years at a junior college. Tired of lecturing and longing for a change, she decided to try working at a different level in the educational system. The public schools were not hiring, so she accepted a job with a small, conservative, church-affiliated school at a considerable reduction in salary, even though she was neither conservative nor religious. She agreed to teach four sections of freshman history and one of remedial junior English, a total of 143 students.

Janet found teaching high school to be challenging and exciting. She liked being with the students and even relished lunchroom duty, for it afforded her the opportunity to observe student interaction. Accustomed to dealing with adults and high-school graduates, she treated her students with respect and genuine care. In a short time she developed an easy relationship with her classes and became known as an adult who could be approached. Janet made a habit of coming to work early every day in order to be available for those students who wanted to shoot the breeze or needed to talk seriously. There was usually someone waiting for her, occasionally a student other than her own or even a fellow teacher.

Much as she loved and was rewarded by her work, she found dealing with the school's administration to be very difficult. Janet's philosophy of education emphasized discovery, opening the world for the student. She attempted to create a proper relaxed atmosphere for this. The school's position stressed adherence to rules and strict norms of acceptable behavior. She had a difficult relationship with the principal and the attendance secretary, both of whom, she felt, should never have been allowed near children. Janet had observed that neither person seemed to like or trust people, and they were unpleasantly manipulative in their handling of others. Both had indicated to Janet that they found her relationships with students to be unprofessional because she did not maintain a proper distance.

Janet believed that the administration's views adversely affected the rest of the faculty and the student body, as well as herself. No one was given any freedom or responsibility at all.

Each classroom had a two-way speaker, and it was known that the principal and the attendance secretary occasionally listened to class sessions. On the third day of school, Janet had been called on the carpet for allowing excessive noise in her classroom. When she apologized to her neighbors, she discovered that the complaint had not come from them but from the attendance secretary, who had been eavesdropping on the public-address system.

During faculty meetings, Janet had pointed out .the need for a student lounge and had suggested the creation of a mutual-help program in which students could tutor each other. She was told that students could not be left to themselves and could not be trusted.

Janet faced a year at a school where she was often in direct opposition to administrative goals and philosophy. It was a time of great stress, during which she had to make and defend many difficult decisions. Two cases will illustrate Janet's dilemma.

## Case One

Janet's relationship with her remedial English class is a very special one indeed. They have been put in a remedial group because not one of them cares a whit for school. From the very first day Janet has made it her most important priority to help them build self-confidence and develop a positive attitude toward their work. She believes that they will learn only when they want to learn and that that can happen only when they feel good about themselves. As a result of the atmosphere that Janet creates, discussions are frank and challenging. Reading books like *The Bell Jar, Flowers for Algernon,* and *The Pigman* provides ample fuel for discussion, and the class spends a good part of the year reading and writing poetry. Janet is pleased and proud to note improvement in both depth of thought and the level of articulation among the students.

Several weeks after Christmas vacation, a discussion arises in class about rules and their necessity. Before Janet is able to react, the discussion moves toward an intense protest against school policy, including personal criticism of the principal and the attendance secretary. The discussion becomes vociferous and emotional, the students venting three years of frustration and anger. Feelings become so intense that Janet can only sit back and let the storm pass. Then she is faced with a series of very difficult questions, the first of which is posed by one of her students: "Ms. Wyler," the student asks, looking at Janet with obvious trust and respect, "what's your opinion?"

*Some Questions*

1.  Often teachers find themselves not in total agreement with a school policy or not very impressed with the leadership skills of a principal. Would it be wrong to share these opinions with students? If you were Janet, what would you say to the students in this case, and how would you justify your decision?
2.  Is this a case of surveillance or supervison? Could you construct arguments for and against the policy of monitoring classes by twoway speakers? Which argument carries the most weight? Why?

## Case Two

Janet teaches history across the hall from the freshman English class, which is taught by Mr. Burry. John Burry, known affectionately as Burry, or Furry

Burry when he is sporting his winter beard, is an explosive, charming, funny, and very popular teacher. The boys think he is terrific, and many girls have a crush on him. This is so despite the fact that he is considered one of the toughest teachers at the school. Freshmen are known to dread Burry's tests two weeks in advance, and he has one of the highest proportions of failing grades in the school. He and Janet share a deep affection for the children, a lunch period, and off-beat senses of humor. Janet has observed him teach and has learned from him. She likes and respects him. They plan to experiment during the last month of school and teach as a team, synthesizing the two disciplines and mixing their classes.

It is a shock to Janet when she hears several uncomplimentary things about Mr. Burry. She is approached by the entire honors section of the history class and is told a tale indicating that he is guilty of insensitivity, unfairness, temper tantrums, and racial prejudice. Janet finds the accusations hard to believe, but the students are adamant, and one is near tears. They claim that Burry threw a book at a student. They saw it. Another student says that Mr. Burry called him a "Chink." The class is agitated and upset. Janet realizes that their emotions are real and that they feel persecuted by Burry. She finds this hard to believe, but she must deal with this. She respects Mr. Burry as a teacher and likes him very much as a person. She is already committed to work with him. Obviously his class is not being monitored by the administration. What can she do?

*Some Questions*

1. Does Janet have a right to renege on her agreement to team teach with Mr. Burry? What would be just cause for doing so in this case?
2. Are there issues of due process in this case? Even if. true, does the evidence students present make a case for the presence of racial prejudice in Mr. Burry's class?


## COLLEGE OR WORKFORCE?

Central High School is the sole secondary school for Iron City, an aging northeastern industrial town. Iron City has seen better days and suffers from many of the problems that afflict our older towns, but Central High School has continued to serve the townspeople in the face of changing economics, demographics, and vocational aspirations.

Two facts about Iron City's population are important for any analysis of the school's place in the life of the town. Some residents of Iron City, Irish and Polish workers who have been in the mills and shops for generations, have great hopes for their children. They want them to make a better life by attending college and escaping the life of the mills. In recent years, their wishes on the subject have been reflected in an increased commitment to academic counseling and college preparatory courses at Central High School.

Another group has also had great impact on the town and the school. During the last twenty years large numbers of Latin Americans have arrived in Iron City, and their presence has affected the cultural life of the town and the educational mission of the schools. Central High School has sought to ease the process of assimilation for this group by emphasizing language instruction and instituting courses in cultural history. Yet, in the great melting pot, some things do remain the same. These Hispanic students now hold places in vocational education classes that formerly had been filled by first-generation Irish and Polish youngsters.

Norman Anderson, the principal of Central High School, has been satisfied with this state of affairs. He feels that the school provides an adequate, sometimes excellent, education for its students and serves the town in a suitable manner. The curriculum is balanced in such a way that it allows each student to pursue individual needs and interests, and the guidance department takes an active role in the process of selection. The rising numbers of graduates who attend college has been a source of pride for Mr. Anderson.

Given these perceptions, it is not surprising that Mr. Anderson has had some difficulty understanding the complaints of Mrs. Virginia Cruz, the mother of a sophomore student at the school. According to Mrs. Cruz, her son, Dennis, has been treated unfairly by his guidance counselor. Dennis Cruz intends to continue his education after high school and wishes to register for college preparatory courses. However, his adviser, Mrs. Kennedy, does not think that he will do well in these courses and has recommended that he register for the vocational education program instead. In Mrs. Cruz's opinion, the adviser has no right to turn Dennis away from his dreams at such an early age, when many other students are given a fair chance. In fact, she feels that this is an example of Mrs. Kennedy's prejudice. Mrs. Cruz has observed that a disproportionate number of Hispanic students are enrolled in vocational education courses at Central High School, and more often than not, they are advised to apply for apprenticeships or join the armed forces upon graduation, rather than apply for college admission. Mrs. Cruz believes that these practices should cease, for they are implicitly racist and discouraging to her son. He should receive the same sort of education and encouragement as other students. She will pursue this matter in a more assertive manner unless her son's wishes are acknowledged.

Mr. Anderson requested a conference with Mrs. Catherine Kennedy, the head of the guidance department, in order to discuss this question. She has informed him that her decision is not a matter of prejudice at all. Rather, her recommendations are the result of a realistic and objective evaluation of the student's chances for academic and vocational success.

Dennis Cruz has not been a top student, and his grades and test scores support this conclusion. Like many Hispanic students, he does not possess the language skills and cultural background that would enable him to do well in college. In Mrs. Kennedy's opinion, she would be remiss in her responsibility as an educator to say or do otherwise. Furthermore, the financial burdens of higher education would be too great for the parents to bear. It would be unfair to recommend any other course of action and leave Dennis Cruz unprepared for those situations that he will have to face in the workaday world. Besides, the existing system has been the path to success for other immigrant groups, and it is probably the best policy to pursue at this time.

*Some Questions*

1.  In this case, both perceptions and concepts of fairness are in conflict. It is obvious that the school official and the parent perceive the present situation differently. Is this an example of prejudice or a realistic view of the way things work in a heterogeneous society?
2.  Should the application of this principle of equality of opportunity be extended to include open access to training and higher education for all? How might Mrs. Cruz and Mrs. Kennedy argue their respective positions with each other?
3.  Should the school serve as society's sorting mechanism?

## VALUES CLARIFICATION

Tom Henderson teaches at Central High School in Kenton, a small exurban community about thirty-five miles from a major metropolitan center. Long unaffected by the tempo and changes of modern life, Kenton is now in the midst of transition from a sleepy rural town to a sophisticated satellite city of the emerging high-tech economy. The landscape presents an incongruous blend of farms and research laboratories, and residents work at occupations that range from dairy farming to computer programming.

After reading a series of books on the subject, Tom decided to develop and teach a unit in values clarification. It went over very well with the students, and each time he presented it he found that the students became more receptive to the subject and their discussions became increasingly earnest and wide ranging. Eventually, Tom designed and offered an entire course called "Decision Making," which he hoped would help the youngsters to sort out their own beliefs and autonomous lifestyles. The course involved role playing, sensitivity encounters, questionnaires, and other strategies taken from the literature on the subject. The curriculum committee of the local board of education approved the course.

The central idea of the "Decision Making" course is that a person creates his/her own values through decisions. We must choose our own values by our words and actions, free, as much as is possible, from authority, conditioning, and social pressures. Only in this way do values become authentically our own. There is no way to prejudge situations, and no other person can really tell us what is right or wrong. Tom uses realistic exercises concerning such subjects as lifeboat ethics and food shortages to press home his point. He is not so much concerned that his students come up with pat answers as he is that they immerse themselves in problematic situations that test and stretch their beliefs.

Some of the parents were surprised by the new topics of dinner table conversation that their children brought home from school, and some became annoyed at the orientation of the course. In their opinion these exercises served to confuse and destroy values, not clarify them. They claimed that the course was the exact opposite of what wholesome moral guidance should be. For example, one parent complained that her daughter had told her that stealing could be justified under certain circumstances. So, she said, if her child "chose freely" to steal because she thought that it was justified by the situation, who would sit with her in juvenile court, the school? In the end, who is to be responsible for the values children learn while growing up, and whose desires are to determine school policy on these matters?

Another criticism was that the endless sequence of games and questionnaires tended to place the trivial and the profound on the same level. For example, one survey asked these sorts of questions:

> Do you enjoy watching television?
> Do you enjoy attending church or synagogue?
> Do you prefer the country or the city?
> Do you like baseball?

It was as if baseball and religion were assumed to hold the same degree of importance in a person's life; possibly not, if one preferred one over the other. It did not seem to make much difference in this approach. How were the parents to inculcate cherished values and emphasize the importance of a hierarchy of beliefs in life, if these beliefs were treated as subjects for surveys and role playing that were all on the same level? Kenton used to be an orderly town in which people knew what was right and how to act, but the rush into modern times was washing all that away. What was so bad about the old-fashioned morality that it needed to be clarified?

After much complaining and parental pressure, the director of guidance, Tom Henderson, and several other teachers who advocated the new approach met with the parents in a stormy PTA session. Their primary defense was that they saw themselves not as inculcating new values or destroying the old morality but as engaging in an effort to teach students to think for themselves and to identify clearly the values that their parents, churches, and society have already established as important. Nevertheless, the parents continued to oppose the course, saying that the family, not the school, was the proper forum for exploring morality and that the course should be dropped from the curriculum.

This case presents a quandary for those who are interested in the relation of ethics, moral education, and the school. Many people complain that the schools have become amoral or immoral and that they should become more concerned with inculcating values. However, when this is attempted it is often said that the schools espouse the wrong morality or that they should not be involved in this activity at all.

*Some Questions*

1.  Should schools be engaged in moral education?
2.  Is moral education the teaching of a code of ethics, values clarification, teaching how to reason objectively about ethical decision making, or creating a caring and just environment? Some, all, or other than these? What are the differences between them?
3.  How would you approach the teaching of ethics in your classes?

## ABUSE? NEGLECT? OR NOTHING TO WORRY ABOUT?

After class, Mary Sue came to Ms. Broudy looking a little frightened. She confessed that perhaps she shouldn't be doing this to her friend, but she was worried about her and had to tell somebody. It seems that when Mary Sue and her friend Kim were at a sleepover together on the weekend, Kim showed her some cuts on her lower arm and told her that she couldn't stand it at home anymore. It had something to do with her father, but she wouldn't say what it was. Mary Sue was worried that Kim might be being molested or beaten or maybe even inflicting wounds on herself as a prelude to suicide.

Ms. Broudy assured Mary Sue that she would speak to Kim and go to the school counselor if things really were as bad as Mary Sue had said. The next day Ms. Broudy asked Kim to stay at the end of class. She asked Kim if everything was all right at home. Kim said it was fine. She asked if she got along with her father, who was a principal of an elementary school in the district. Kim blushed and said, of course. But when Ms. Broudy asked to see Kim's arms, she refused to show them, saying it was personal and none of her business. Ms. Broudy did notice Band-Aids on the inside of both of Kim's wrists, but Kim just said it was poison ivy. Did she need help in any way? Kim said, "No."

Ms. Broudy had some doubts. There was a clear school policy that even the mere suspicion of child abuse must be reported to the school counselor and principal. Ms. Broudy didn't hesitate. She went to both and told them the whole story. The principal knew Kim's father as a fellow principal and just laughed. He couldn't believe anything like that of him. The counselor said she would talk to Kim.

A week passed. Kim seemed to get even more distant in class and one day appeared with a bruise on her cheek. Ms. Broudy went to the counselor to find out what had happened with Kim's interview. The counselor said in her professional opinion there was nothing solid she could report to the authorities. She had called the parents to see what they thought was going on at home. The mother had nothing to say The father said Kim was just being moody and would grow out of it.

Ms. Broudy returned to her room to find Mary Sue. Mary Sue was crying. She said Kim had finally told her that her father had abused her. Kim was getting desperate. Mary Sue was worried that she might do something to herself.

*Some Questions*

1. What would you do if you were Ms. Broudy?
2. If this turns out not to be a case of child abuse, is it possibly a case of child neglect? Were the parents neglecting the clear signs that Kim was having serious problems? Is there a difference between neglect and abuse? Does a teacher or the school have any obligation to report child neglect? To whom?
3. Is due process a consideration in delicate cases of possible child abuse or neglect? Wouldn't strict adherence to due process disfavor the child?
4. Do/should parents have the right to physically strike their children?
5. Do/should teachers have the right to physically restrain students?

## FRIENDLY SUPPORT OR SEXUAL HARASSMENT?

It had happened again. She felt very uncomfortable, but maybe it was all in her mind. Maria Sanchez was in her third probationary year at Bonnville high school. Her tenure decision was in process, and Mr. Alsop, her department chair, kept her informed of its progress as best he could given the confidentiality required by school policy.

Maria was a modestly good teacher of social studies. Her subject matter background was a little thin in European history, and she had worked hard to improve it. She had a few discipline problems in two of her firstyear classes, but that too, had improved. All but one of her bi-yearly evaluations were satisfactory. She thought she had a good chance to earn tenure.

She needed the strong support of Mr. Alsop, though, and there was the problem. Many of the women teachers talked about his insensitivity. He sometimes would tell off-color jokes at department meetings without a clue that some women blushed. In public, he would put his arm around male and female teachers alike in gestures of fun and colleagueship, but sometimes a little fondling would seem to go on. Rumor had it that he slept around a lot. Some women said he made their skin crawl. But he was a good, efficient chair of the social studies department, and his judgment was respected by the administration.

Maria felt a little intimidated by him. Maybe it was her imagination, but it seemed that ever since this year began, Mr. Alsop managed to sit next to her at faculty and department meetings; his knee would gently touch hers; sometimes in a gesture of comfort he would pat the back of her hand; sometimes he would just look at her longingly and smile.

When they met in his office in March to discuss how her tenure review was going, he made it clear that he had to keep certain things confidential, but that he was the kind who with a good dinner and wine sometimes told more than he should. He wondered if they could have dinner together. They could discuss European history, teaching, and school politics. Nothing personal of course! Except perhaps her tenure review.

He reached for her hand and said, "Please? Tonight?"

*Some Questions*

1. Do you think Maria had reason to feel uncomfortable? Is feeling uncomfortable the same as being sexually harassed?
2. What kinds of things constitute sexual harassment in a school setting?
3. Do you think every school should have a policy against sexual harassment? If yes, what should it be and what procedures should be provided to enforce it? If no, why?

## GRADING POLICIES

David Levine is the chairperson of the social studies department at Henry Hudson High School, a large metropolitan secondary school. Because of the size of the student population, several sections of certain courses are offered each year, and each is taught by a different instructor. In the case of modern American history, three teachers offer courses. Students are assigned to these courses according to a simple alphabetical rotation. This simple system has become a complex problem for Mr. Levine.

The first section is taught by Albert Foley. Mr. Foley is a young, somewhat idealistic teacher who believes that stimulating learning experiences form the core of an education. In his class, he relies upon the study of current events from newspapers and television, and he encourages his students to initiate independent study projects. Mr. Foley is not as much concerned about command of exact facts as he is about the personal significance that modern American history may come to hold for his students. In that direction, he believes, lies the promise of good citizenship. He grades students on the basis of essays about topics they select and journals of personal response to classroom discussion and current events. Among the students, he is known as "Easy A" Foley. In a typical year, thirty percent of his students will receive A's, and another thirty percent will receive B's. The rest are given C's, with an occasional D for serious cases. Mr. Foley says that a student will pass his class if he is able to find his way to the classroom. In his opinion, it is hard enough being a teenager, and he is not going to make it any tougher. He believes that his children really learn and grow in their sense of self-worth because of his policy.

"The facts and nothing but the facts" might be the motto of William Sampson, the teacher of the second section, for he believes that subject matter is all important. Mr. Sampson relies on the textbook exclusively, and he delivers very detailed lectures. He demands that his students know the facts about American government and recent historical events, and he has very little patience with uninformed opinion. In his view, good citizenship must rest upon a solid foundation of knowledge. He tells his students that they must learn American history backwards and forwards, or they will not pass his course. In order to guarantee this, the students must take rigorous objective examinations that test their knowledge of the most exact matters of fact. In a recent class of forty students, the grades were distributed in the following manner: three A's, five B's, eighteen C's, nine D's, and five F's. Mr. Sampson contends that his tests are fair measures of his students' knowledge. The students call him "Slasher Sampson."

Nancy Wright, the teacher of the third section, believes that life is a competition for finite resources, and her course is taught in a manner that reflects that belief. In the future, her students will have to struggle for pieces of the pie at the table of life. Similarly, in her classroom, they must compete among themselves for places in a hierarchy of achievement, for Ms. Wright grades according to a curve. In her most recent group of forty students there were five A's, ten B's, fifteen C's, seven D's, and three F's, a distribution of grades that she has come to favor after some experience. Ms. Wright uses both essays and objective tests in order to provide some unbiased basis for her judgments. She believes that her proportional approach to grading avoids questions of favoritism and accurately reflects the performance of each student as it compares to that of others in the class. Ms. Wright's students have no nickname for her.

Mr. Levine, the department chairperson, has had many complaints from parents, students, and other teachers about this state of affairs. Each teacher has been criticized on grounds of fairness. According to these critics, the performance of any one student, as measured by the final grade, will vary with the policy of the teacher. It seems that the grades of many students in modern American history depend upon the luck of the draw that originally places them in their respective classes. This is a form of random selection, an attempt to avoid partiality, but is it fair?

*Some Questions*

1. This case reflects a common educational practice, giving freedom to teachers to structure their own classes and devise their own grading systems. Obviously this can create unequal treatment of students in different sections of the same course or across the same grade level. Should grading procedures be standardized? What would be some arguments for and against standardization?
2. Imagine being each of these teachers in turn-Mr. Foley, Mr. Sampson, and Ms. Wright. How would you defend your approach to grading? How would you respond to Mr. Levine if he told you he thought your approach to teaching American history and your grading system were unfair?
3. Should there be limits on the freedom of teachers to design and carry out their courses in the way they independently judge to be best? On what grounds might such freedom be limited? On what principles

# Additional Resources

Bricker, David. *Classroom as Civic Education.* New York: Teachers College Press, 1989.
> Bricker argues that cooperative learning and more emphasis on community are essential to the achievement of the goals of a liberal society.

Brighouse, Harry. *School Choice and Social Justice.* New York: Oxford University Press, 2000.
> A normative discussion of school choice that emphasizes the centrality of autonomy and equality.

Callan, Eamonn. *Creating Citizens: Political Education and Liberal Democracy.* New York: Oxford University Press, 1997.
> An excellent discussion of the connection between political theory and education for citizenship.

Curren, Randall. *Aristotle on the Necessity of Public Education.* Oxford, England: Rowman and Littlefield, 2000.
> A look at the moral basis of public education by means of a discussion of Aristotle.

Curren, Randall, ed. *A Companion to the Philosophy of Education.* Oxford: Blackwell, 2003.
> This excellent collection contains a variety of articles on ethical issues in education.

Fischer, Louis, David Schimmel, and Leslie R. Stellman. *Teachers and the Law.* 6 ed. Boston: Allyn and Bacon, 2003.
> A fine textbook discussing the law as it applies to teaching.

Goodlad, John; Soder, Roger; and Sirotnik, Kenneth. *The Moral Dimensions of Teaching.* San Francisco: Jossey-Bass, 1990. ✓
> A collection of essays emphasizing the importance of the moral in an adequate conception of teaching.

Hansen, David T. Exploring the Moral Heart of Teaching. New York: Teachers College Press, 2001. ✓
> A rich historical, philosophical account that takes us to the moral heart of teaching.

Howe, Kenneth R. *Understanding Equal Educational Opportunity.* New York: Teachers College Press, 1997.
    A thorough discussion of equality of opportunity.

✓ Nash, Robert J. *"Real World" Ethics: Frameworks for Educators and Human Service Professionals,* 2nd ed. New York: Teachers College Press, 2002.
    Describes three moral "languages" practitioners can use to deal with ethical issues in everyday situations.

Peters, R. S. *Ethics and Education.* London: George Allen & Unwin, 1970.
    A classic discussion of several ethical concepts, such as punishment and equality, in an educational context.

Rawls, John. *A Theory of Justice.* Cambridge, MA: Harvard University Press, 1971.
    This book is one of the most important works in philosophy in the 20th Century. It is the classic statement of the concept of justice as fairness.

Schulte, John M., and Cochrane, Donald B. *Ethics in School Counseling.* New York: Teachers College Press, 1995.
    A discussion of the ethical issues that arise in the context of counseling.

Sockett, Hugh. *The Moral Base for Teacher Professionalism.* New York: Teachers College Press, 1993.
    A discussion of the moral basis of teaching as a profession.

Strike, Kenneth. *Educational Policy and the Just Society.* Urbana: University of Illinois Press, 1982.
    A discussion of the concepts of liberty, equality, and rationality as applied to a range of educational problems.

Strike, Kenneth A.; Anderson, Melissa; Curren, Randall; van Geel, Tyll; Pritchard, Ivor; and Robertson, Emily. *Ethical Standards of the American Educational Research Association: Cases and Commentary.* Washington, DC: American Educational Research Association, 2002.
    A discussion of research ethics rooted in AERA's code of ethics and employing a case method.

Strike, Kenneth; Haller, Emil; and Soltis, Jonas. *The Ethics of School Administration,* 2nd Ed. New York: Teachers College Press, 1998.
    A discussion of ethical issues in school administration. The book is modeled on *The Ethics of Teaching.*

Strike, Kenneth A., and Moss, Pamela A. *Ethics and College Student Life.* Boston: Allyn & Bacon, 2003.
    A book on ethics for college students, using cases, with discussions of topics such as cheating, tolerance, and sex.

Strike, Kenneth A. "The Ethics of Resource Allocation." In *Microlevel School Finance,* edited by David H. Monk and Julie Underwood, 143-80. Cambridge, Massachusetts: Ballinger Publishing Company, 1988.

This article discusses ethical issues that concern the distribution of educational resources.

Strike, Kenneth A. The Ethics of Educational Evaluation. In the *New Handbook of Teacher Evaluation: Assessing Elementary and Secondary School Teachers.* Edited by Jason Millman and Linda Darling-Hammond. Newbury Park, CA: Sage, 1990.

A discussion of the ethics of teacher evaluation.

Strike, Kenneth A. "Against "Values"." *Educational Policy Analysis* 1, no. 13 (1993).

This article argues that the term "values" is dysfunction because it blurs important distinctions and encourages excessive subjectivity in ethics.

Strike, Kenneth A. "Discourse Ethics and Restructuring." In *Philosophy of Education, 1994,* edited by Michael Katz, 1-14. Urbana, Illinois: Philosophy of Education Society, 1995.

This article discusses the implications of discourse ethics for school governance.

Strike, Kenneth A. "The Moral Responsibilities of Educators." In *Handbook of Research on Teacher Education, 2nd Ed.,* edited by Thomas J. Buttery and Edith Guyton, 869-92. New York: Macmillan, 1996.

A discussion of the role of teachers in promoting citizenship.

Strike, Kenneth A. Ethical Leadership in Schools: Creating Community in an Environment of Accountability. Thousand Oaks, CA: Corwin Press, 2006.

This book discusses a range of issues in the ethics of leadership with an emphasis on community and accountability.

Tamir, Yael. "Education and the Politics of Identity." In *A Companion to the Philosophy of Education,* edited by Randall Curren, 501-08. Oxford: Blackwell, 2003.

A discussion of identity politics in education.

White, Patricia. *Civic Virtues and Public Schooling: Educating Citizens for a Democratic Society.* New York: Teachers College Press, 1996.

A pluralistic democracy needs certain virtues and values to hold it together. White describes the role of the school in nurturing the democratic virtues of Hope, Confidence, Courage, Self-respect, Self-esteem, Friendship, Trust, Honesty, and Decency.

Zubay, Bongsoon , and Jonas F. Soltis, eds. *Creating the Ethical School: A Book of Case Studies.* New York: Teachers College Press, 2005.

A set of cases concerned with ethics in schools.might it be defended?